ERWIN BAUER'S
WILD ALASKA

ERWIN BAUER'S WILD

ALASKA

Photos by Erwin and Peggy Bauer

Base maps by Joe LeMonnier

Published by Outdoor Life Books

DANBURY, CONNECTICUT

Published by
  Outdoor Life Books
  Grolier Book Clubs Inc.
  Sherman Turnpike
  Danbury, CT 06816

Distributed to the trade by
  Stackpole Books
  Cameron and Kelker Streets
  Harrisburg, PA 17105

Produced by Soderstrom Publishing Group Inc.
Book design by Nai Chang
Typography by David E. Seham Associates Inc.
Text face: 10/12 Goudy Old Style

Library of Congress Cataloging-in-Publication Data

Bauer, Erwin A.
  Erwin Bauer's wild Alaska.

  Includes index.
  1. Alaska—Description and travel—1981–
2. Alaska—Description and travel—1981–   —Views.
3. Natural history—Alaska. 4. Outdoor life —Alaska.
5. Bauer, Erwin A.—Journeys—Alaska. I. Bauer, Peggy.
II. Title.   III. Title: Wild Alaska.
F910.5.B38   1988   917.98'045   88–28883
ISBN 1–55654–046–9

Contents

Preface

Writing a book is no easy task for someone who grows restless when-ever trapped indoors for very long. But I found the writing easier and more enjoyable for this book on Alaska than for any of my previous books. Each day's research would help me recall pleasant events, spec-tacular places, golden days, and people who became good friends. You will meet many of these friends throughout this book. Alaska is simply a grand place to visit now and savor in memory.

From nowhere else do so many interesting, occasionally bizarre, news stories originate. Soon after I began composing the first chapter, on the morning before April Fool's Day, a fish collided with an Alaska Airlines Boeing 727 jet. It seems the regularly scheduled flight was taking off from Juneau airport and had barely cleared the runway when its flight path crossed that of a bald eagle carrying a fish in its talons. The terrified bird dropped its catch, which fell and left a dent and imbedded scales in the plane.

While writing one of the early chapters in this book, I read that commercial fisherman Travis Murphy was working on the stern of a boat in Kodiak Harbor when fellow crewmen saw him suddenly disap-pear overboard. A sea lion had grabbed him by the behind and pulled him about six feet underwater before letting go. Just playful, maybe. Or trying to get even.

Then I read that the current global warming trend was causing gla-ciers in Southeast Alaska to advance with amazing speed. Taku Gla-cier, for instance, has been advancing the length of two football fields each year. Scientists predicted that Hubbard Glacier, which damned Russell Fiord in 1985 with a sudden advance, would do so again soon, trapping many marine mammals and maybe some people, too.

Continuing my work, I read about camp cook Larry Hadselford, of the El Cap Gold Mine near Ketchikan, hurrying to use a brand new outhouse. Inside he looked down the hole into the eye of a black bear that had trapped itself below and was unhappy with the situation. Quickly back outside, Hadselford found four friends to help move the structure so the bruin could escape.

And how about 70-year-old Kathleen McCann of Ninilchik? She went fishing in Cook Inlet and caught what she figured was a new world-record Pacific halibut. At 466 pounds, the prize was 16 pounds heavier than the existing record. But when the fish was disqualified because of a rusty, "inadequate" scale, McCann said she didn't give a hoot. "Just seeing that fish cavort and fight and you wouldn't care, either," she explained.

As I was finishing the writing, there arrived both good and bad news from Alaska. The killing of wolves from helicopters was can-celled, I hope forever, for budget reasons. That's the good news. But the divorce rate was running much higher than the national average because in too many marriages the spouses were not equally fond of living in the 49th State. In fact an Anchorage preacher declared that the whole state was too uncivilized—unfit for man.

Fortunately for wildlife, a great many people everywhere agree with that preacher's assessment. Some of us though realize that there is no splendid wilderness of equal size anywhere to match Alaska. Many of us want to save and maintain Alaska in just this uncivilized condition for future generations to explore and enjoy.

Too many others, I fear, see Alaska as a resource to be exploited, a wild land to conquer, no matter what the consequences. They are not at all worried that the chainsaw is systematically cutting down the old rain forests of Southeast. I hope this book, this labor of love, will convert some of those who would consume Alaska and that they will instead join Peggy and me in trying to preserve it.

Erwin A. Bauer
Jackson Hole, Wyoming

7

Salmon-colored sunsets such as this have probably illuminated the Yukon Delta region
in western Alaska since the dawn of time.

INTRODUCTION

The Eighth Continent?

One magical night, when first contemplating a book about wild Alaska, I sat alone outside a rude sheep-hunting camp in the Wrangell Mountains, trying to assemble my thoughts. That soon became totally impossible because of what appeared in the cold, clear September sky: It was a night of the aurora borealis impossible to forget.

At first there was only a streak or an arc of white light, glowing, like a reflection of the indistinct snowy ridges all around. Gradually the light became more and more intense, extending from horizon to horizon. Finally a greenish glow seemed to hang from the entire northern sky like a shroud, pulsating, wavering, growing dim and pale, pink and blue, then exploding into brilliance again. According to some scientists and some Indians on lonely traplines, I should also have heard the aurora, a sound like the rustling of silk or perhaps the stirring of the night wind. But I couldn't, maybe because my hearing is poor. The spectacle alone was powerful and intimidating.

In baffling language, geophysicists theorize that the aurora is really billions upon billions of particles charged by the sun, battering and at times penetrating the earth's shield. Some Eskimos regard it much more simply. According to one legend, this stunning night display is caused by spirits of the dead bowling with a giant walrus skull, generating sparks. Another legend claims it is a cold fire burning in heaven to light the way for lost souls. No matter, because the eerie experience made it easy for me to imagine that I was witnessing the birth of Alaska. I gave up my own vigil that night only when frost crystals began to form on my parka and the deepening cold drove me shivering inside my tent and into a sleeping bag. Still, I couldn't sleep for a long time. The shimmering, unearthly glow was visible even through the thin tent walls.

The aurora borealis did indeed illuminate the night skies when Alaska was "born," during the Cretaceous period about 125 million years ago. At that time large, shifting, drifting sections, or plates, of the earth's crust collided, joined, and thereby gave Alaska its outline and major land features. Ever since, the state's surface has been shaped, tortured, or sculpted to a large degree by retreating and advancing glaciers, by volcanoes, and by violent earthquakes. Between 1788 and 1961 some 880 earthquakes measuring 5.0 or more on the Richter scale occurred in Alaska.

On Good Friday afternoon, March 27, 1964, residents were reminded of the Great Land's instability when one of history's greatest earthquakes occurred, centered in south central Alaska. It caused a half-million-square-mile area to shudder and crack. Measuring 8.6 on the Richter scale, it was twice as violent as the 1906 earthquake that leveled San Francisco. Far more than 114 would have been killed if the quake had happened on a school and business day, rather than on a holiday. The fact that property damages reached a billion dollars seems insignificant when compared to the fact that a whole coastal area tilted while, in a few minutes, an enormous land mass and sea bottom shifted westward twenty feet or more horizontally, toward the Gulf of Alaska.

THE BERING SEA LAND BRIDGE. As recently as 30,000 years ago, Asia was connected via Alaska to North America by a vast grassland that supported large numbers of grazing animals. This area is now known as the Bering Sea Land Bridge.

Most magnificent among the free-roaming mammals on this land bridge was a shaggy herbivore with long, coarse hair that grew beyond the woollike coat that grew close to its skin. Weighing many tons and with ivory tusks that may have measured 10 feet, wooly mammoths were giants roaming in the Pleistocene era. It is only in the permafrost soil from arctic Canada across Alaska to Siberia that remains of the mammoths (as well as other Pleistocene fauna and flora) have been preserved, fast frozen and/or buried, sometimes remarkably intact.

The Bering Sea Land Bridge, once beneath the seas,

ARCTIC CIRCLE

BERING SEA LAND BRIDGE

Big Diomede Island
Little Diomede Island

Noatak River

BR

AL

BERING SEA

Yukon River

Lake Iliamna

KATMAI
NATIONAL
PARK

Kodiak
Island

ALEUTIAN ISLANDS

Barrow

ARCTIC NATIONAL
WILDLIFE REFUGE

BROOKS RANGE

GATES OF THE ARCTIC
NATIONAL PARK

N. Fk. Koyukuk R.

YUKON TERRITORY

N.W.T.

ALASKA

Fairbanks

Mt. McKinley

WRANGELL
MOUNTAINS

ST. ELIAS MTS.

Yukutat

GLACIER BAY
NATIONAL PARK

P A N H A N D L E

Admiralty Island

B.C.

GULF OF ALASKA

Ketchikan

was exposed when the oceans retreated. This permitted the first humans to reach North America as they followed the wild animals they hunted and on which they subsisted. It is now apparent that the ancestors of the Aleuts and Alaskan Eskimos were among the last humans to make the crossing from Asia before the land bridge was again submerged beneath rising seas at the end of the last Ice Age. This occurred between 10,000 and 12,000 years ago.

When the land bridge disappeared, so did the wooly mammoth, the wooly rhinoceros, the cave lion, and other grassland creatures. Warmer temperatures changed the vegetation and may have done so very abruptly. The cool, lush, grassy steppe that had extended well into Alaska beyond the land bridge had provided pasture for mammoths and their allies. Now it was altered to bog and tundra, laced with lakes in summer and snow-packed in winter. The ancient species could no longer survive.

From remains discovered during the last century we know that the mammoths perished by several different means: from starvation and being smothered beneath landslides, from being trapped or isolated by the changing course of glacial rivers, or from plunging to their death when eroded lakeshores collapsed under their great weight. Some wildlife species were able to adapt and survive, and many of these appear later in this book.

STELLER AND THE BERING EXPEDITIONS.
More than a hundred centuries after the last wooly mammoth expired, the next humans ventured from Asia to Alaska. And this time they came across open, often angry, seas.

These men belonged to the crew of Vitus Bering, a Dane, who in 1728 was commissioned by Czar Peter the Great of Russia to see if Russia and North America *were* still connected by land. No doubt poorly equipped, Bering cruised northward from Kamchatka, Siberia, in a small sailing ship. Without ever seeing the Alaskan coast through the clinging fog, Bering returned after only two months with the report that the two continents were separate.

Neither the czar nor anyone else in St. Petersburg, then Russia's capital, was convinced of the truth of this, so Bering was instructed to make a second, more thorough, investigation. This time he needed 13 years to prepare for the voyage. He returned to Siberia and built two square-rigged ships, *St. Peter* and *St. Paul,* equipped both, and finally set sail once again in 1741.

Only a few hundred miles at sea, the two tiny vessels were permanently separated in rain and dense fog. A month later Bering and his men on the *St. Peter* had

a first glimpse of the New World when the overcast lifted briefly to reveal the white peaks of what we now call the St. Elias Mountains. With his mission thus accomplished, Bering felt vindicated and was again ready to turn back. It may have been Georg Wilhelm Steller, a German staff member on board, who persuaded the captain to anchor and go ashore on a nearby Alaskan island for fresh water.

Steller was a young botanist sent on the *St. Peter* to describe any new land the expedition might discover, as well as to document and collect its plant and animal life. But Bering had no sympathy for Steller or his mission and allowed the scientist only 10 hours, or the time necessary to fill wooden water casks, on that one unknown (today) island.

Steller never did set foot on the Alaskan mainland.

Steller's sea lions are silhouetted in late summer on satellite rocks off Kodiak Island.

But he furiously collected as many plants and birds as time permitted. One of the birds was the handsome blue-black jay still abundant along the southeastern Alaska coast (and in my own backyard), known today as Steller's jay.

Botanist Georg Wilhelm Steller sighted sea otters (above) on his ill-fated voyage with explorer Vitus Bering. The best place I've found for seeing them is Afognak Island. Steller also saw fur seals, shown on the facing page.

Later, en route homeward, a violent North Pacific storm blew the *St. Peter* aground, marooning the crew on another island near Siberia. While the rest of the men fought just to stay alive through the bitter winter, suffering from scurvy, exposure, and malnutrition, Steller escaped illness by eating the green plants he found and urged others to do so. Some did, but 30 men, including Vitus Bering, died. This predicament did give Steller a chance to study and collect some of the strange life-forms and to make field notes, while at the same time nursing the ailing sailors and burying the dead on the lonely island.

Among the animals Steller found were sea otters, fur seals, and sea cows. More about the first two mammals later in this book. The sea cow was a huge, sluggish, and docile relative of the manatee and dugong, both of which are warm-water, even tropical, creatures. An adult sea cow measuring about 25 feet long probably weighed about 10 tons, making it the largest species of its order, Sirenia, and larger than many of the world's whales.

It is possible that the entire world population of sea cows may never have exceeded 1,500 individuals and that all or most lived on only two of the Commander Islands—Bering Island (where Steller was shipwrecked) and Cooper Island—but no one really knows. Bones have recently been found on two of the western Aleutian Islands. Unfortunately, the Steller's sea cow was not only edible, a source of nutritious meat and sweet-tasting fat, it was also easy to catch. It lived in shallow, in-shore gardens of kelp, and teams of seamen found it easy to spear and manhandle ashore.

Nobody knows exactly when the last sea cow was dragged onto a North Pacific beach and there carved up to feed Russian crews, but it happened before another professional naturalist, or scientist, was able to examine one, dead or alive. When the 46 survivors of the *St. Peter* built a small boat from the wreckage of the old to sail back to Siberia, the botanist Steller was able only to carry along a few dried seeds and the unique horny plates that were the "teeth" of the sea cow.

On arrival Steller's notes and pitifully few specimens were shipped from Kamchatka to St. Petersburg, but he never saw his published observations because he

Inhabiting many of the bays, coves, and splendid fiords of southeastern Alaska, the spotted harbor seal ranges southward to California.

died during a Siberian winter at the age of 37, far from home and family in Germany. Soon his grave was robbed and then was washed away altogether during the following spring by a rampaging river. Absolutely everything we know or ever will know about the extinct sea cow came from this one lonely botanist.

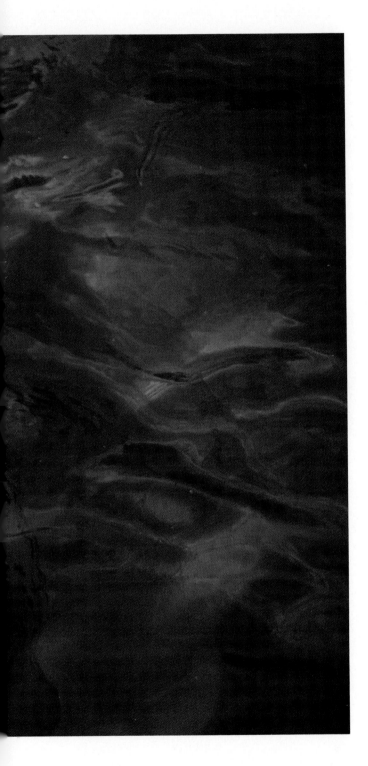

St. Paul, commanded by one Alexei Chirikov, continued onward and in one month the scurvy-ridden, filthy, hungry crew did reach and anchor somewhere off mainland Alaska, maybe near where the town of Yakutat lies today. Immediately a longboat with 10 sailors was sent ashore for fresh water and to reconnoiter, but they never returned. A second and last longboat was then sent with six men to search for the first group. They also vanished forever.

Now with freshwater reserves desperately low, and no more boats left to go ashore on a forbidding distant land, Chirikov and the remaining crew watched in fear as two colorful, decorated craft full of "savages," also decorated and painted, rowed out to within "three cable lengths" of the ship. There they regarded the invaders for a while in silence before paddling back into the mists along the shore. Chirikov had to draw the melancholy conclusion that he would never see his sailors or longboats again and thus had only one option, to return as quickly as possible to Siberia.

Unfortunately for his career and ambitions, Chirikov had encountered the Tlingit Indians of southeastern Alaska, a prosperous and independent people (whose ancestors had also originated in Russia) who doggedly resisted the Russians for the next hundred years. In the long run, the Indians lost. But their resistance was only the first example of the problems and dangers that adventurers and early explorers of wild Alaska would have to endure. Yet even though the Indians were formidable, the weather and terrain proved to be greater problems.

In fact Alaskan waters are the graveyards for more Russian ships and their crews than history records. In the decades after Bering, more Russians came to the new land that promised fantastic fortunes from trade in wild furs. Despite the hardships, hunger, and even death that were then ingredients of North Pacific travel, the prospects for lucrative trade triggered the first exploitation of the Great Land. Following Bering and Chirikov came the Promyshlenniki, the same freebooters and plunderers who had slaughtered fur-bearing animals across the Asian steppes into Siberia. Only now they hunted from ships. Among their first hunting grounds were the Aleutian Islands.

Unlike the Tlingits, the native Aleuts were quickly enslaved and treated with a brutality uncommon even for those harsh times. Entire Aleut villages were held hostage while the men were forced to work as guides and hunters in the systematic slaughter of marine mammals that almost sent many species the same way as Steller's sea cow. We are lucky that most have rebounded and are part of wild Alaska's treasure today. The Russians of the 1700s never developed an interest in the frigid interior and northern regions of Alaska.

Loss of the wooly mammoth could not have been avoided. But that of the sea cow could have been. It is extremely sad that extermination of Steller's sea cow came at the hand of humans.

Now let's return to June 1741. Remember that the two ships of Bering's "fleet" were separated at sea soon after the start of the voyage. The second ship, the

From Homer and across Kamishak Bay, the Kenai Mountains often look shrouded.

Because of this they missed out on the gold and other ores that later adventurers would find.

THE ALASKAN TERRAIN. I always have a hard time describing the magnitude, the variety, and the overwhelming, haunting beauty of Alaska. Nor is it easy to convey the size of the state, which is one-fifth that of the continental United States, 20 times the size of Rhode Island, and larger than the next three largest states combined: California, Texas, and Montana. Its 365 million acres spread over 31 degrees of latitude and 43 degrees of longitude, about the same distance east to west (2,400 miles) as from Savannah, Georgia, to San Diego. North to south (Barrow to Ketchikan) equals the distance from northern Minnesota to Charleston, South Carolina. If you started out to explore the coastline of this, one of the world's largest peninsulas, you would have to cover 94 miles a day, every day, for a year to cover the entire 34,000 miles of shoreline. No wonder it has been called the Eighth Continent.

Yet as I write this, Alaska's human population is fewer than 500,000, with more than half living in a few larger cities. Only one person exists for every 8 square miles of land, which is 40 times more elbow room than the average citizen has elsewhere in the United States.

An Alaskan or a visitor has 3 million lakes to explore, each over 20 acres. One lake, Iliamna, is the second largest in the United States, yet is little known outside the state. A person could climb 15 mountain peaks (including Mt. McKinley, the highest on the continent) higher than any in the other 49 states. One of Alaska's 5,000 glaciers is larger than Switzerland. The interior is drained by great river systems, including the Yukon, North America's third largest. It rises in Canada's Yukon Territory and flows 2,000 miles to empty into the Bering Sea on the western Alaskan coast. Floating, exploring, studying, savoring, fishing the Yukon's full length could be the experience of a lifetime.

The westernmost point of Alaska, Little Diomede Island, is also the closest point to the Soviet Union. The channel separating it from Big Diomede Island, a Soviet territory, is only 3 miles wide.

The terrain of Alaska is every bit as awesome as its immense size. Approximately a third lies at low elevation and is flat enough to slow the Yukon and other great rivers, where they meander and unwind through vast expanses of tundra and muskeg. Here

During the long days of summer, fireweed illuminates roadsides throughout Alaska.

on these flats in high summertime, tens of thousands of seasonal "thaw" lakes gleam in the sunshine. A traveler sees a lot more of the sun over the flat interior than he does along the coastline.

The rest of Alaska is mountainous, ranging from rolling foothills to peaks that are too seldom seen through or above the overcast. It is the mountain scenery I find most overwhelming. I have wandered widely in the Rockies, not so widely in the Himalayas and southern Andes. But for sheer, numbing grandeur Alaska's mountains win out.

With good reason the Brooks Range of north central Alaska has been called the primal heart of the state. Geologists generally agree that this distant, sublime real estate is the true, the original Alaska, with all the rest attached later by continental drift. Stretching east to west from border to border above the Arctic Circle, this 37-million-acre elemental wilderness broods beneath continuous daylight for a month each summer. This is one rare place in the world where, with a map under one arm and a pack on your back, you can still explore landscapes no one else has ever seen.

Most of the Brooks Range has no road access whatever, no trails, no guided nature walks, in fact nothing to help or guide a visitor. Streams, lesser peaks, and valleys are not even being named anymore by personnel of Gates of the Arctic National Park. From the air, which is the only way anyone can reach this park, the land appears smooth and green, but that is very deceptive. What you are really seeing is a morass of tussock grasses growing over permafrost in clumps too tall for anything except an adult moose to cross easily. Elsewhere are terrible alder thickets, a few of which shelter grizzly bears. But neither tussocks nor alders nor bruins can match the impact of the sometimes living atmosphere of insects when the wind dies: deer flies, no-see-ums, and especially mosquitos. However, the rewards for perseverance are total solitude and unspoiled, unrivaled beauty.

There are two ways to explore the Brooks Range without all the agony. One is to climb quickly out of the valleys and into the foothills where bugs and ground obstacles are fewer. Better still, because the entire range is laced with clear, cold, sapphire rivers, explore by canoe or inflatable raft. Best known of the Brooks Range rivers are the Noatak and the North Fork of the Koyukuk.

I should mention another unseen dimension of Alaskan terrain: Here some of the most impressive

No animal contributes more to the mystique and awe of wild Alaska than the grizzly bear of the Interior. This sow and her cub symbolize wildness in America.

seismic zones on earth cause the land mass to plunge sharply to enormous depths offshore. For example, the Aleutian Trench lies as deep as 25,000 feet below sea level. Thus Alaska contains both the highest and lowest points on the continent, with a vertical difference of 9 miles between the peak of Mt. McKinley and the base of the Aleutian Trench.

Alaska includes about 1,800 named islands, but there are many more that have not been officially named. The 10 largest islands each contain more than 1,000 square miles. Biggest of all is Kodiak, home of the largest bears, which has 3,588 square miles. Admiralty, where the *most* bears live, is just half that size.

The state has 18 wildlife refuges, of which the Arctic National Wildlife Refuge is the most extensive (3.8 million acres). Add to these Katmai and Glacier Bay national parks, the two largest in the United States and among the largest in the world. Few natural and no man-made wonders anywhere begin to rival them.

Maybe more than its remoteness and ruggedness, Alaska's climate has kept the Great Land in relative wilderness. That climate ranges from temperate to frigid or worse, and from extreme localized dryness to nearly continuous rain- or snowfall. Although situated close to the Arctic ice pack and even nearer the North Pole, Barrow (Alaska's northernmost community) is not as cold as Fairbanks or most other places in the interior. The southernmost point in the Aleutian Islands (and in Alaska) is at nearly the same latitude as London, England, and has a similar damp, often foggy climate. Annual rainfall in the southeastern Panhandle varies from heavy to the heaviest in the United States. Conditions just half way up 20,320-foot Mt. McKinley are as severe as that at the North Pole. Even in July, temperatures regularly fall to minus 30°F, and wind gusts might exceed 70 miles per hour.

Dall, or white, sheep live on Polychrome Pass in the Alaska Range, as they have since migrating there from Asia over the Bering Sea Land Bridge.

A land so far north of the equator, so cold on the average, could not possibly contain the genetic diversity of warmer wilderness areas. Still, Alaska is home to a surprisingly rich and abundant fauna and flora. More than 1,500 plant species have been cataloged, including trees, shrubs, flowers, ferns, grasses, and sedges. (By comparison, more than that number have been counted on a single acre of tropical rain forest in Brazil.) The farther from the equator, the fewer species are able to survive, although total numbers (or mass) of these few may be great indeed.

Alaska's wildflowers tend to be small and delicate rather than large and gaudy, as in the tropics. The tundra and alpine regions are especially rich in blooms during spring and summer. The state flower is the forget-me-not, *Myosotis alpestris*. This is a very widespread and exquisite plant with bright blue petals surrounding tiny yellow eyes. Forget-me-not seems an especially good choice for a state which, after the first visit, is itself impossible to forget.

CHAPTER ONE
Adventure Road North

Late one afternoon in early July in 1955, northwest of Dawson Creek, British Columbia, I turned off the gravel, washboard road and parked at one side of a level clearing. Although not designated an official campsite, the spot had been heavily used by campers. In fact several families traveling together had already pitched their tents at the opposite end of the clearing. There a cold stream emerged from the dark evergreen forest. Exhausted from a long day of driving a rough, potholed roadway, always pursued by clouds of dense brown dust, I felt relieved just to turn off the ignition.

My first chore was to exchange a rear wheel for one of the spares I carried. The tire had developed a slow leak and was partially flat. Next I erected a heavy green canvas tent purchased long before through a Sears & Roebuck catalog. It had neither the sewn-in floor nor the screened windows and entrance of today's models. After pumping up an old Coleman stove, I placed a pot of water on it to boil for coffee and in the creek splashed the road dirt from my body. How refreshing that felt! Finally I sat down and leaned against a bedroll to savor the cool northern twilight. But the peace and quiet didn't last long.

Suddenly a small black bear appeared in the clearing not far from the neighboring tenters. Immediately, and I suppose naturally, the cub became the center of attention, and somebody started to toss it slices of bread. That's bad business of course. The next thing I knew, the cub's mother was on the scene.

Assessing the situation quickly, she growled and sent the cub running away. Then she walked directly toward the tailgate of a station wagon where all the food for an evening meal had been spread. The bear either ate or managed to clear away most of the banquet before being angrily driven off by men throwing rocks and one swinging a shovel.

Naively I figured we had seen the last of that bruin. Right after eating my own dinner, I crawled into my sleeping bag. Asleep almost before I could zip the bag

Above: A black bear cub only a few months older than this one caused my first fretful night along the Alaska highway. Previous page: My earlier trips up the highway were dust choked and tough on tires, but the 1520-mile highway is mostly paved now. Overleaf: For many, the drive from the lower 48 states begins in Montana, near Glacier National Park and Swiftcurrent Lake.

up, I was wide awake again in what seemed only minutes later. Now in the darkness people were shouting, clanging pans together, and someone blew a car horn insistently. The bears were back, unmindful of the soft rain that had begun some time earlier.

When the noise subsided at the other side of the clearing, I could hear the animals scratching outside not far from my own tent. I sat up in a cold sweat, my sleeping bag gathered around my middle. Although

at the time I'd had no experience with campground bears, I had locked all my food inside the car. I fervently wished I were locked inside with it. Fortunately, the bears wandered off without investigating my tent. But it was a very long night.

When I broke camp, daybreak was still only a pale promise in the eastern sky. I haphazardly loaded my gear, and before breakfast headed northwest again on the Alaska Highway. I certainly didn't feel rested. But be thankful for small favors, I thought; the rain had settled the dust.

Not far down the road I came upon a small cargo trailer that had been abandoned and the wheels removed. Somebody had painted on the rear: "This road is misery, turn back now." Just a little farther along someone else had erected a crude sign that read: "Sinners repent. HE is coming soon. Welcome to the Alaska Highway."

In 1987, over 30 years later, Peggy and I drove the Alaska Highway again, this time southeastward—homeward toward Wyoming—and I tried to find that old camping place again where the bears had wrecked my sleep. But either my memory was faulty or the

place no longer existed, because that section of road had been relocated. But searching for it certainly revived memories of another time.

Despite my inauspicious start in 1955, that first venture into Alaska was a trip of pure wonder and discovery. I had long dreamed of visiting that wild territory. No young man ever read more about the Great Land than I did. Then Alaska was not a state yet, and I would write about the trip for *Outdoor Life.*

At that time I did not keep detailed notes as I have since, and must now rely on memory alone. But I do clearly remember seeing my first Stone sheep, a slate gray subspecies of the Dall sheep which is white, as I rounded a sharp bend near Muncho Lake in British Columbia, where black bears also haunted a popular camping site. Travelers were not very careful in those days about leaving garbage, so I soon learned that bears could be expected at almost every regularly used place.

At that time Whitehorse, the Yukon capital, was virtually the only community of any size between Dawson Creek, where the Alaska Highway officially began, and Fairbanks, Alaska, where it ended. I

One of the few places to see Stone sheep in the wild is around Muncho Lake, British Columbia, on the southern portion of the Alaska Highway.

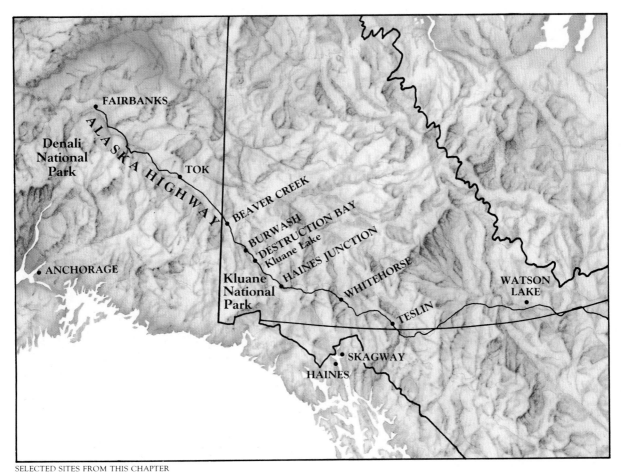

SELECTED SITES FROM THIS CHAPTER

Today, essential services along the highway are available at reasonably close intervals.

paused in Whitehorse to have several inner tubes patched and to buy staple groceries. The repair work was fairly cheap, but the food was very expensive. Early the next morning, near where a paved road now branches northward toward Dawson City (*not* Dawson Creek) and the old Klondike goldfields, the first wild wolves I'd ever seen ran across the gravel road just ahead. There were three of them. Later that day I studied my first white sheep through binoculars high above the road and overlooking Kluane Lake in what today is Kluane National Park.

Now, as then, the place names along the Alaska Highway have a magical, exciting ring to my ears: Fort St. John and Fort Nelson, Pink Mountain and Prophet River, Toad and Liard rivers, Liard Hot Springs, Watson Lake and Teslin, Burwash, and Destruction Bay, Beaver Creek and Port Alcan. Just studying a map is enough to infect a young man (as well as the same much older one today and his wife) with acute wanderlust for exploring wild places. Two weeks after leaving Columbus, Ohio, on that first trip I finally arrived in Tok, just inside Alaska. In 1987,

Peggy and I covered a similar distance, without really pushing hard, in half that time.

Tok exemplifies the great change that has taken place in three decades. There one fork of the crossroad led to Fairbanks, the other to Anchorage. At the crossroad was a gas station, an auto repair garage (where tire repair went on around the clock), and a few crude tourist cabins. Today in summer Tok is a busy small town with a choice of service stations and attractive motels, a visitor center, RV parks, a supermarket, a small museum, and a fine fragrant bakery.

BUILDING THE ALASKA HIGHWAY. Construction of the winding ribbon of road, then called the Alcan, was something of an engineering marvel. Work began in March 1942, four months after the attack on Pearl Harbor, and required only eight frantic months to complete 1,542 miles of road. Until then, no overland route had existed across the raw wilderness from the United States to Alaska, its remote northwest territory. Because of early Japanese military successes in the Pacific (the Japanese would even oc-

27

cupy islands in the Aleutians for a while), the United States feared that travel by sea to Alaska might be cut off. So a road was deemed necessary to supply U.S. troops there. Though actually finished in October 1942, the Alcan was not always easily passable. And winter locked up the major portion, which was within Canada. Formal dedication of the road took place during a November blizzard at Soldier's Summit, Yukon, as the first military convoy rolled north.

Such a colossal undertaking in so brief a time required an extraordinary amount of men, materiel and earth-moving equipment, all quickly assembled. Because speed of construction was considered the overriding factor, the Alaska Highway was never noted for its expertly engineered course. Crews toiled around the clock during the short summer of 1942 to complete as much as 3 or 4 miles a day over muskeg and low mountain passes, across deep canyons and wide glacial rivers. With hindsight, it's apparent that the engineers did not always take the best possible routes.

Road builders, many unfamiliar with such formidable terrain, had to remove millions of tons of topsoil and muskeg, replacing it with gravel, which would usually disappear when roadbeds thawed at the end of winter. The first few springtime road breakups usually occurred along stretches of quagmire where a fair road had existed the previous fall. Add to quagmire the steep grades and sharp curves, and you have a hazardous road even when passable.

Few towns of any size existed in that Alaska–Canada border wilderness, so the influx of workmen had immense impact. A post office employee in Whitehorse, site of a major construction camp, remembers processing mail for about 350 residents, then being responsible for 10,000 people a month or so later.

The civilian and military Canadians and Americans who worked on the Alaska Highway have characterized the experience as unforgettable. More than any other factor, probably, they will remember the incredible abundance of wildlife—in the form of dense clouds of mosquitos. Bears also became a nuisance but were nothing compared to the insects of June. More than once on my own first trip up the Alaska Highway, I endured nightmare nights with the hummers, trying to sleep in an unscreened tent with nothing but a thick application of Oil of Citronella on my skin. Fortunately, like the highway itself, the quality of insect repellents has been miraculously improved since that time.

Maybe a poem sent by an unknown reader to the Fairbanks Daily News-Miner, and widely reprinted during the late 1940s, best symbolizes the original Alaska Highway:

The Alaska Highway winding in and winding out,
fills my mind with serious doubt,
as to whether the lout who planned this route
was going to hell or coming out.

As it turned out, the highway was never of strategic value to the military because the faster, handier Inside Passage sea routes to Alaska were never threatened. But soon after World War II ended, civilians found its value. They probed tentatively farther and farther north on what became one of the greatest adventure roads on earth, bisecting one of the finest surviving wilderness areas.

THE ALASKA HIGHWAY TODAY. Gradually every summer since World War II the highway has been improved by grading, rerouting and widening, and by upgrading bridges. Now there are 1,200 paved miles of the 1,520-mile total. Some of the paving is recent and extremely smooth going. Even the unpaved sections are well maintained and nothing like the ordeal of the unpaved road in 1955.

In reality the Alaska Highway is now almost anybody's challenge because communities have sprung up at intervals along the right-of-way. We found most essential services for modern travelers to be available every 50 miles or so and often much closer. We could buy anything from propane, bread, and canned goods to fishing licenses, diesel fuel, unleaded gas, and locally made Indian moccasins at one-hour driving intervals from start to finish.

Today there are alternatives to catching the highway in Dawson Creek, which remains the best bet for travelers coming from the eastern two-thirds of the United States and eastern Canada. A bonus is to aim northward from Great Falls, Montana, to Calgary, Alberta (and the junction with the Trans Canada Highway), then north again through the incomparable Canadian national parks of Banff and Jasper to Prince George, Alberta, and then Dawson Creek.

Americans living along the Pacific Coast can drive directly to Prince George, then west toward Prince Rupert, British Columbia, and finally due north on the new, mostly paved Cassiar Highway that joins the Alaska Highway midway at Watson Lake.

Still another and recommended alternative is to board one of the frequent car ferry boats (which I'll describe in the next chapter) at Seattle or at Prince Rupert, BC, and, via the Inside Passage, travel the marine route to Haines or Skagway, Alaska. Excellent paved roads connect Haines with Haines Junction, Yukon, and Skagway with Whitehorse, both of which are on the Alaska Highway.

Dall sheep are visible along the highway in Kluane National Park, Yukon, at Mile 1029.

We have driven those last two connecting roads many times and each has led to great adventure. But I must make one important point: Although it passes from Dawson Creek to Fairbanks mostly through brooding wilderness where northern wildlife lives, the Alaska Highway is not always the ideal avenue for seeing great numbers of wildlife, as many contend. If you are already traveling at daybreak, or remain on the road until dusk and later, your chances of seeing wild creatures increase. But the animals along the highway are simply more wary than in national parks, in Denali for example. Nor can a traveler stop at just any stream or lake along the way, no matter how enticing it seems, and expect to fill a stringer quickly with fish for dinner. Most of the waters do contain lake trout, grayling, whitefish, northern pike or some combination, but you have to work to catch them. Yet if you canoe or hike some distance from the traffic, beyond the beaten track, you really can find bonanza fishing.

Distances along the Alaska Highway were originally marked and indicated on road maps with mileposts (or, nowadays, in Canada, in kilometer posts), but most of the original concrete markers are gone. The distances are no longer exactly accurate because of straightening and relocation of sections of the road. But designations such as Mile 555 or Mile 871 are still used to indicate a roadhouse or certain stream crossing, a historical marker, or an abandoned silver mine. I have paused each time since my first trip at Mile 1029, in the Yukon.

At Mile 1029, the Highway forms the eastern boundary of Canada's Kluane National Park. On the opposite side of the road is 157-square-mile Kluane Lake, which the Highway parallels for about 40 miles. The steep slopes of the St. Elias Mountains (within Kluane Park) on the west side of the road at Mile 1029 are important winter range for a large band of Dall sheep because high winds keep the area fairly free of snow. Until about mid-June in springtime, when the sheep move to higher, greener pastures elsewhere, and again after mid-August, I have always seen the white forms of Dall sheep above the road, and occasionally even beside it.

Late in May 1986, Peggy and I counted almost 50 sheep, many ewes with very young lambs, when we stopped to study the slopes through binoculars. That day the air was crisp and sunny, perfect for climbing

This is one of the few grizzlies I have seen along the highway.
But grizzlies are present in many places, so campsites should be kept
clean, with edibles stored out of reach.

and photography. So we decided to try for pictures of the animals.

Many mountains look deceptively easy to climb, depending on where you stand below, and this was one of them. The nearest band of about a dozen ewes and lambs appeared to be quite close, but we needed about an hour to reach their level and then to scramble slightly above them. There we mounted cameras with telephoto lenses onto tripods before beginning a cautious, slow approach. Since the animals here on Sheep Mountain are somewhat accustomed to humans, they paid little attention as we came into good range where a female nursing a lamb completely filled our viewfinders. A band of five young rams watched us from an outcropping of rock about 100 yards directly above.

After a time, the ewes and lambs wandered to a ledge where they bedded down and soon were nodding. It was warm, and we later stopped photographing to sit and soak up the warm sunshine while admiring the magnificent Yukon scene. Feeling very lazy, even sleepy, I may have dozed for a short time when Peggy jabbed me hard in the ribs to wake me. She pointed to a place far up on the slope behind us, well beyond

where the young rams were quickly leaving their bedding places in alarm. I could hear rocks rolling downhill from far above them and see the white sheep scattering. A moment later I saw the reason. A dark grizzly appeared and then disappeared into a rocky draw.

"Let's get back to the road," I said. In a surprisingly short time we were standing again by our van. A ranger, Terry Hoggins of the Canadian Park Service, drove up to join us. He told us an interesting story of bear predation on sheep that was just then taking place.

Only days before, on May 17th, Hoggins watched a grizzly approach a ewe with a newborn lamb in almost the same place we had been sitting in the sunshine. The ewe ran for the safety of a cliff that loomed over the Alaska Highway. Unable to follow, the lamb instead ran downhill where the bear easily caught it, carried it back upslope into brush, and ate it. Two hours later Hoggins saw the same bruin rush into another band of sheep, but this time all escaped.

Ranger Hoggins said that early the next morning the dark grizzly caught a second lamb on Sheep Mountain and quickly ate it, too. Hoggins estimates that both the lambs caught were about four or five days old at most, each a meal at one sitting. Then while we were talking with the ranger, the 400-pound bear made still another attack, the fourth actually witnessed. But the terrain prevented us from seeing whether the griz was successful or not. Perhaps significantly, the bear did not soon emerge into view to continue hunting.

The bear's strategy was a simple one—to walk past and above a female and very young lamb while not seeming to notice them. Suddenly the grizzly would rush downhill, sometimes successfully. It seemed that this particular grizzly had learned how to make a good living, at least during the brief lambing season, in a traditional Dall sheep lambing area. In a very short time any normally healthy lambs would have been

able to evade such attacks, and maybe the bear was well aware of that.

We camped in the area of Mile 1029 for two more days in case of any further action but did not see that bear again. Life among the sheep groups seemed peaceful as always.

CAMPING. It is true that traveling to Alaska via the highway can be almost as expensive as traveling by sea or air, because the long distances make it time-consuming. But the cost is not without great compensation and a few bargains. By far the biggest bargain along the way is the camping, no matter whether you pitch a tent every night or go by self-contained recreational vehicle. Campgrounds are numerous

I shot this camping scene, including my son Bob,
along the Alaska Highway in the 1960s. Today the wilderness scene is the
same; only the camping equipment has changed.

enough now, well-spaced along the way. They are kept clean and tidy and are seldom filled. Recently, campsites in the Yukon Territory were only about $5 Canadian per night (about $4 U.S.). Within Alaska, campgrounds in the state park system are free. Because of policing, sanitation, and better manners of campers, bears today are a novelty more than an expected nuisance. But we did meet campers who had just "survived" an unsettling encounter with a campground invader.

As usual on retiring to their tent one night, they locked all edibles in their car, out of reach of animals. Everything, that is, except the tube of toothpaste they had left on a wooden picnic table. In the morning they heard shuffling just outside the tent and looked through a window into the face of a coal black bear that seemed to be frothing white at the mouth and grimacing as if mad. Only later did they find the toothpaste tube now ripped open. Apparently the bear did not relish the taste because the bruin didn't come back.

The first public campground a traveler finds, heading northwestward and on entering Alaska (where the Alaska Highway becomes Alaska Route 2), is Deadman Lake State Recreation Area at Mile 1249. It has

been such an attractive stopover for us that it is worth describing.

One cool evening, we arrived early enough to have our choice of the 16 wooded sites, some of which were close beside Deadman Lake. We parked our van on the most level spot and then walked along water's edge where we found a good many shorebirds feeding and resting in the grassy shallows. Returning from the van with a camera and tripod, we managed to approach a certain lesser yellowlegs closer than we'd ever been able to before. The photos we got are among our favorites. The last sound I heard before falling asleep that night was the haunting serenade of nearby loons.

Deadman Lake, another camper told me, contains northern pike and it was obviously the perfect weedy lake for exploring and fishing by canoe, though we had no canoe. But using waders instead, I rigged up a spinning rod and soon caught a three- or four-pound pike, called a jack locally. That's far from bragging size, but was just right for a memorable breakfast. Afterward I tried casting again, but without luck.

The area around the campground is a good first opportunity to get acquainted with permafrost, a condition that exists over a large portion of the world's

Mallards flush from many of the wetlands the highway crosses.

32

arctic and subarctic regions. Within the permafrost belt or limit, which forms an irregular line across northern Canada and Alaska, only the top layer of ground thaws in summertime. The earth below this remains permanently frozen. At Deadman campground, the first evidence of permafrost is the rough, upheaved entrance road leading from the Alaska Highway to the lakeshore. Traffic has so compacted the ground in warm weather, exposing tree roots on both sides, that the trees themselves now lean inward toward the center to form a peaked entrance arch.

More noticeable still is the way that concrete fireplaces at campsites have sunk from 1 to 2 feet straight down. The heat from the cooking fires causes the permafrost beneath to melt and the concrete pads then settle farther and farther. Curiously, permafrost has had exactly the opposite effect on the pit-type toilets. The action of frost has actually raised the base of the privies upward a few inches every winter. As a result, camp maintenance workers must occasionally add a new step to each outhouse stairway.

Although far from the super-smooth, high-speed thoroughfare Americans are used to in the Lower 48, the Alaska Highway is far more remarkable. It leads

Especially in autumn, golden eagles are often perched or flying along the Alaska Highway. Below: In spring, male willow ptarmigan patrol the roadsides. All are changing plumage from winter white to summer brown.

to and through the kinds of wild lands that are so rapidly vanishing elsewhere on earth. The roadway heads toward wild Alaska. There every serious outdoors enthusiast has a last chance to escape to adventure, if only for a little while.

CHAPTER TWO
Southeast Alaska and the Marine Highway

By early evening the ocean tide was in full flood, and a ripline had formed just off the shore of Bell Island. Past one isolated rock, the current raced fast enough to form a rapids as turbulent as any on an inland wilderness river. Herring gulls skittered across the surface, and a pair of bald eagles circled overhead. Guillemots and auklets gathered to dive and catch fish all around us. This was a beautiful scene.

"Let's move in a little closer," I suggested to my buddy Herb Shaub, "and let the boat drift along the edge of the rip."

Herb turned the craft toward shore. When he felt the surge of the tide, he shifted the outboard into neutral. With fishing tackle already rigged, we tossed two herring baits overboard and watched them dissolve into the cold, emerald water. Line evaporated from our reels.

For a few moments the baits and our boat were swept along in the current. Herb checked the drag on an old reel and I turned to watch one of the eagles, which had caught a fish and now glided to shore to eat it. Gulls swooped down to rob the huge white-headed bird. That's when I felt a thump on my line, followed by a stronger thump, and next heard the whine of my reel. Raising the rod tip instinctively, I set the hook.

Forty yards away a salmon cartwheeled out of the water. An instant later it raced away toward Asia. "Better use the motor," I said, "or we may never see this one again."

Herb reached for the gearshift lever on the outboard but didn't quite make it. At that same instant a salmon struck his bait and darted away in the same direction as mine.

What followed might have been comical for some-

Beached at low tide, an angler holds up a salmon just taken off Bell Island. Previous page: Nowhere in the world are bald eagles more common than along the scenic coastline of southeastern Alaska. Look for the magnificent raptors at any season.

body else to watch. While the tide towed our boat in one direction, two salmon were heading the other way, sometimes in and sometimes out of the water. Monofilament line peeling from the reel burned my thumb. By holding his rod tip high overhead in one hand, Herb managed to keep our lines from fouling when they crossed—twice—and at the same time managed to shift the outboard into forward with his other hand. And none too soon.

SELECTED SITES FROM THIS CHAPTER

We began to regain line, but it wasn't easy. Luckily the salmon did not choose to run deep and instead cruised near the surface, jumping or porpoising. Finally I netted mine and then Herb's. A moment later I was holding up a pair of fat and silvery humpback salmon, the first of the species I had ever seen. They weighed about 7 pounds apiece.

And that was only the beginning. Throughout that long, unreal southeastern Alaskan twilight of early July 1968, which lasted until nearly midnight, we enjoyed almost continual action. Most of it was furnished by the humpbacks, or pink, salmon which seemed to haunt the tidal rip. But we also boated a pair of chinooks—king salmon—one of them weighing 38 pounds. When a salmon did not strike, and our baits drifted too close to the bottom, we hooked sole, tomcod, or rockfish. Our largest fish was a halibut. This one was about all I could handle on the same plugcasting outfit I intended for much smaller game in freshwater lakes. Except for the halibut, which when fresh may be the best fish I have ever eaten, we released all.

If my fishing tale sounds fictional, I guarantee it is not. Nor was that fishing hole a secret. Its steep hills covered with evergreen rain forest, Bell Island is about 50 miles from Ketchikan, Alaska's southernmost city and at the head of the Behm Canal. The Behm is not really a canal, but a long, narrow, deep, fiordlike portion of the Inside Passage.

Except for the small resort community of Bell Island Hot Springs, built on stilts where steaming Bell Island Creek gushes out of a hillside, the island is uninhabited and surrounded by wilderness. Considering that the region of Bell Island and nearby Yes Bay are often surrounded by gamefish, it surprisingly remains one of Alaska's least known treasures. King salmon begin running there in May, and some still linger into July.

36

All communities of southeastern Alaska are tied together by auto ferries of the Alaska Marine Highway system, extending south to Seattle.

Silver, or coho, salmon appear late in the summer. In between you can catch humpbacks and dog, or chum, salmon. Yet Bell Island offers only one sample of the considerable adventure I have found in southeastern Alaska.

THE PANHANDLE. Southeast, often called the Panhandle, is that narrow strip of coastal and mountain real estate that extends southeastward from the main body of Alaska, toward the Pacific northwestern states. Flanking British Columbia, it runs southward

from the town of Yakutat and includes Sitka, Glacier Bay National Park, Wrangell, Juneau (the capital), Misty Fiords National Monument, and Ketchikan. It terminates at Cape Fox near the mouth of the Portland Canal.

This is a region of mountains drained by waterfalls and of towering evergreen forests rising beside giant glaciers that flow to the sea. A mosaic of thousands of green islands separates the mainland from the Pacific Ocean, making it possible to travel the entire length of the Panhandle between the shoreline and the sheltering islands. This waterway is known as the Inside Passage.

My fishing friend Herb Shaub observed that there were two kinds of weather in Southeast: the "normal" wet kind that makes the area as green and exquisite as it is, and the sunny kind that you desperately hope to encounter. The usual rainy, or at least gray and misty, weather makes the rarer sunny days especially appreciated. June is the driest month here, and October is the wettest.

More rain falls in the southern part of the Panhandle than in the north. It rains so much in Ketch-

Bunchberries are among the many fruits found in the dark green coastal forests.

ikan—an average of 13½ feet a year—that residents grimly keep score. In 1949 a record 17 feet fell on the town and its environs. There is a barometer on top of Deer Mountain, about 3,000 feet above Ketchikan, which is at sea level. "If you cannot see the

Left: The most common large mammals of the Alaskan Panhandle are Sitka blacktail deer. In the damp evergreen forests, blacktails are tough to spot and photograph.
Above: Lynx live silent as smoke in the lush forests of southeastern Alaska.

peak," locals say, "it's raining. If you somehow *can* see the peak, it is going to rain." More than once when a bright morning suddenly followed several days of gloom, I felt that southeast Alaska was the most scenically beautiful land I had ever seen.

Perhaps surprisingly, Southeast's climate is almost as mild as it is moist. Ocean breezes and the Japan Current hold summertime temperatures at about 60°F. In winter the mercury seldom falls below freezing for very long, but the humidity can be penetrating. Keep in mind that Southeast lies at about the same latitude as Scandinavia, and fresh summer days begin soon after twilight.

THE MARINE HIGHWAY. Maybe the unique and most significant fact about Southeast is that it is not connected by highway with anywhere outside. Nor are the major communities such as Juneau, Ketchikan, and Sitka connected by road with one another, a situation that has helped discourage ruinous development. Once transportation was only by air (often small floatplane) or by boat. But in 1961 that suddenly began to change with the launching of the snub-nosed M/V *Chilkat*, a combination passenger and car ferry boat. Today nine ships comprise a fleet that plies the modern Alaska Marine Highway. Now by vehicle/passenger ferry, and beginning as far south as Seattle,

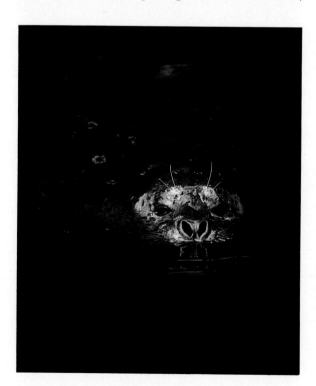

Traveling the Marine Highway, you may be treated to sightings of the spotted harbor seal, which is normally shy of humans.

it is possible to bring your car or camper to several southeastern cities, as well as to Skagway and Haines, which are the gateways to the main part of Alaska farther north.

Ships of the Marine Highway fleet also provide feeder service to outposts of southeastern Alaska: to the Kenai Peninsula, to Kodiak Island, and even to Dutch Harbor in the Aleutian Islands. There is no marine highway or motor vehicle ferry system in the world to match it. Life in and travel to Alaska have been radically changed by it.

The Marine Highway is doubly important to outdoors people because it makes the entire state accessible without the need to drive the greater portion of the Alaska Highway. For two people, from Seattle with a van or camper, it is far cheaper to take the ferry than to fly and then rent a vehicle on arrival. Via car ferry you can carry along all the gear you are likely to need no matter how long your trip. It is also possible to camp—actually pitching tents on a special sheltered deck—aboard the vessels en route. There are also staterooms on the larger ferries making longer runs. And at least in modern times, no ships anywhere cruise through such a magnificent wilderness as the Alaskan Panhandle.

GLACIER BAY. I have often used the Marine Highway to explore Southeast. On one of the most memorable trips with one of my sons, Bob, I disembarked at Juneau and there caught a shuttle flight by floatplane to stunningly spectacular Glacier Bay, then a national monument, now a national park. While we were weighing in duffel and fishing tackle for the short hop, somebody tapped me on the shoulder. The tapper turned out to be Ed Dodd, then creator of the popular cartoon character Mark Trail and owner of the most Southern accent north of Georgia. By coincidence he was also headed for Glacier Bay in search of new material. We decided to join forces.

On a clear day the flight to Glacier Bay is even more revealing of an unspoiled land than the voyage through the Inside Passage. Beginning soon after takeoff we had an eagle's view of the blue-crevassed glaciers that wound snakelike toward salt water and of the sheer ice cliff faces that plunged into the bay. As the plane roared past, great chunks of ice "calved off" glaciers to form a flotilla of icebergs. We could spot harbor seals hauled out on some of the bergs. After making a wide circle, then descending, the pilot glided to a landing at Bartlett Cove, flushing large rafts of white gulls on the approach. Frank Kearns, who managed the Bartlett Cove Lodge, met us at the dock. That evening the three of us joined him in demolishing an extravagant dinner of Dungeness crabs

If you take a day cruise of the Kenai Fiords National Park, out of Seward, you will see hundreds of sea lions hauled out on the rocky shorelines of the Chiswell Islands.

trapped earlier in the day not far from where we sat.

Early the next morning in a fine drizzle, we boarded the M/V *Sea Crest,* a sturdy 64-foot vessel piloted by Captain Howard "Robby" Robinson, who had made a career of vagabonding in Alaskan coastal waters as a commercial fisherman, hunting guide, and outfitter to parties of exploring scientists. He regarded Glacier Bay as the most awesome place in the entire Panhandle, after having poked the reinforced hull of the *Sea Crest* into nearly every remote bay and cove.

From the moment we were free of the dock, where ravens perched and croaked at us, there were no dull moments. Soon we encountered pods of humpback whales, some surfacing several times less than 100 feet from the boat. It was my first, and remains my closest, look at these, among the largest mammals on our planet. When the humpbacks deserted us, they were replaced by Dall and harbor porpoises. One school of porpoises seemed to lead us toward the densely packed icebergs in front of Muir Glacier. These slabs were occupied by hundreds of harbor seals. The seals favor the slabs as pupping grounds. Where else, I wondered, could one watch seals at sea level and white mountain goats on dark cliffs 500 feet above?

Yet for each sea mammal we saw hundreds, maybe thousands, of birds. Northern phalaropes were just then gathering in dense flocks along our cruise path. Skirting the Marble Islands we saw and heard glaucous-winged gulls, marbled murrelets, oystercatchers, pelagic cormorants, black guillemots, and tufted puffins in numbers impossible to census. What a remarkable place for birdwatchers.

The climax of our cruise came when Robby carefully picked his way through blue-green icebergs, some towering taller than the *Sea Crest,* toward the base of Muir Glacier. Robby cut the motor letting us drift freely, so we could hear the constant groaning and grinding of the glacier as it moved toward us. At intervals megatons of ice would break free at water's edge and crash down into the water, close enough to rock the boat.

This constant calving over the past two centuries has caused Muir (and the glaciers connected to it) to retreat more than 60 miles, or an average of 1,700 feet per year. At times the retreat has been a full mile in a single year. It is hard to comprehend that as re-

I shot the Mendenhall Glacier with my son Bob near Auke Bay in the early 1960s. The spot was just as beautiful on my most recent trip.

cently as 1794, when sailing northward through the ice-choked water of Icy Strait, Captain George Vancouver noted only a dent in the shoreline where the entrance to vast Glacier Bay exists today. Great areas of land that were once locked under the glaciers are now being reclaimed by forests and recolonized by a wide range of creatures from yellow warblers and gray-cheeked thrushes to grizzly bears and moose. After our visit near the base of Muir Glacier, the fishing we did for Glacier Bay halibut—good though it was—proved to be an anticlimax.

TOTEM POLES. Imagine for a moment that instead of sailing aboard the *Sea Crest* you are sailing over two centuries ago aboard a Russian trading ship in the wake of George Vancouver. You have crossed the North Pacific to the New World, and now your creaking vessel glides to anchorage in a stony, sheltered cove of southeastern Alaska. Around you is a panorama of mountains, lingering snowfields, and green-black forests shrouded in gray mists. There is also human activity.

A few people are shuffling among the low, rectangular houses that stand beyond the beach. Nearby a fleet of ornate canoes is pulled onto the gravel beach. Racks of red fish hang over dense, smoky fires. Then suddenly, through a brief break in the overcast, you see a row of tall, colored poles that tower like a giant picket fence along the water's edge. Even from a distance it is a puzzling spectacle, a culture shock.

In time you go ashore with the rest of the crew. You inspect the poles at closer range, and they become even more puzzling, if not actually grotesque. On one is carved the image of a grinning human face. Next to it growls a sharp-fanged bear or a toothy beaver or a crab. Wings project from some poles, while others have whale fins or bird beaks. The colors are brick red, black, white, and aqua. Images of humans, birds, fish, and reptiles are stacked, one atop another, 50 feet high and more. What does it all mean?

Few of the Russian merchantmen saw any beauty or significance in the totems. Most were interested only in acquiring a cargo of wild furs, the only apparent riches of this distant land, and then hurrying homeward. Even the well-educated officers barely mentioned the totems in their journals. Some simply reported that the natives—Tlingit and Haida—worshipped wooden idols. Others believed the totems to be mere ornament.

Even until fairly recent times, in fact until midway into the 20th century, relatively few people, Indian or non-Indian, seemed to be interested in this compelling and distinctive art form. Unique in all the world, it evolved and flourished only in the lonely coastal villages of Puget Sound, British Columbia, and Alaska's Panhandle. It also almost died there, totally unnoticed, as the old totems decayed and fell. Few carved new ones and carried on the art. As much as anything else, the Alaska Marine Highway has revived interest in the totems by making the surviving poles accessible to great numbers of people.

The origin of totems and totem carving is almost as mysterious as the carvers themselves. Two hundred years ago the Tlingits and Haidas were few in number and lived in a land of plenty. They could easily thrive on the bounty of the sea and forests that surrounded them.

The earliest totem poles were structural interior house poles, possibly the posts at the corners of the clan houses. The detached and freestanding poles we see today were the last to arrive on the scene and reached their peak of quality and number in the later 1800s. They were fashioned of western red cedar, native to that cool, damp climate. Largely because the natives lacked a written language, totems told a story, even the history of a tribe. Any Indian could read a totem as easily as we read a newspaper.

Carved in cedar by Haida, Tlingit, and Tsimshian Indians along Alaska's Panhandle and coastal British Columbia, totems usually depict wildlife, ancestors, or events.

Most of the figures on totems are easy to identify. Claws, wings, and beaks, of course, represent birds. The straight beak always signified the raven, the most important of the animals. The curved beak was the eagle. Often an entire fish is represented, but just fins or fluted tails can mean the same. Sharp teeth belong to a wolf or bear; look at its feet to see which: long, curved claws are the bear's, rounded paws belong to the wolf. Frogs never have teeth, and the flat halibut with both eyes on the same side of its head is easy to identify. Beavers have recognizable teeth and lifelike scaled tails. Ears of humans are on the sides of the head, those of animals on top.

In some areas where the cedars were notably large, the totems were more massive than those carved where growth produced only small trunks. But no matter how large the pole, its cylindrical shape dictated the general outline of the finished totem.

When the Haida prepared for the carving of the totem pole, they initiated a search for a suitable tree

close to shore. They felled it, cut it to the proper length, and trimmed and peeled it on the spot. If the pole was large and not to be used as a house pole, it was hollowed out on what was to be the back side (the side with more knots). That way, the pole was lighter and easier to move during the carving and raising processes. With the preliminary work completed, the pole was skidded into the water, floated to the village, and beached where the carving was done.

In the early days the carvers used adzes with nephrite jade bits. Later, steel tools brought by the white fur traders were used, including knives with curved blades resembling the Eskimo's *mitlik,* or thumb knife. The carving of a pole took many months, the actual time depending on the number of apprentices hired.

Poles were not lightly conceived or created. Only carvers of known skill were engaged to oversee the making of a new pole. Underlings did the basic work, while the carver attended to the difficult details himself.

Totem poles were usually raised by the trench method. A trench 20 feet long was dug at a 30-degree angle, and the pole was rolled into it, the top at the shallow end. The depth at the deep end was the depth at which the bottom of the pole would rest. This was often shallower than one would expect, owing to the presence of bedrock close to the surface. This is why some poles today lean to one side. A short log roller was placed under the upper end and was moved forward as a team of Indians pulled on ropes attached to it.

Totem poles served several purposes in the culture of the Northwest Coast Indians. There was a ridicule pole, for example. One wonderful ridicule pole holds up to derision a white trader who cheated the Indians in a fur exchange. It stands today at Saxman Park, Ketchikan. In a culture that had no written language, traditions and tribal lore were represented by a totem pole that guided oral transmission. Family histories were preserved in wood. Family crests topped the pole, and the rendering of two crests showed a marriage. Often, too, a pole was made as a memorial to one who died. One famous totem features a top-hatted Abe Lincoln standing at the crown.

There are three major areas in Alaska where you can see totem poles today. One seldom visited by tourists is Klawock Totem Park on Prince of Wales Island. Sitka National Historical Park displays 18 poles

Outdoor poles such as this in Saxman Park, near Ketchikan, reached their peak quality and number in the late 1800s. Earlier totems occurred primarily as corner and center posts of clan houses.

in a beautiful, natural setting along a hiking trail that winds among towering evergreens. Sitka is on a picturesque island southwest of Juneau.

But no doubt the best and easiest place to see many totems of different kinds is in and around Ketchikan. In the center of the town is Chief Johnson's Pole, the only pole still standing in its original position. It was carved and erected there in 1901.

South of Ketchikan on the Tongass Narrows lies Saxman Totem Park, the best place of all to enjoy the totem poles of Alaska in a natural green setting. A spectacular grouping stands in a flat semicircle of grass against the backdrop of deep green forest. On clear days the huge spires can easily be seen from the deck of the car ferries approaching and leaving the busy dock area of Ketchikan.

North of the town is Mud Bight Village, or Totem Bight, the gem of totem collections. Here, on the exact spot where the Tlingit Indians traditionally had a camp, is a marvelous gathering of totem poles carefully placed where each can be appreciated individually. There is also a large Indian clan house built as an exact replica of those constructed before the 20th century. The site is edged by a stream that salmon still ascend to spawn in each year.

THE BEAR MAN OF SOUTHEAST. The story of southeast Alaska, like that of other parts of wild Alaska, is often the story of such colorful individuals as Adolf and Olaus Murie, Georg Steller, Frank Duffresne, and Larry Aumiller. (Aumiller reappears later in this book.) In the southeast our man is Allen Hasselborg, who early in life developed so much suspicion of bureaucracy and civilization that he spent most of his life, the first half of the 20th century, living alone in the wilderness. I never did meet Hasselborg, who died in 1955, but by detouring about 70 miles from Juneau during one Alaska ferry trip, I was able to visit the homestead area where he lived for four decades at Mole Harbor on the eastern shore of Admiralty Island. Admiralty today, as probably for centuries, contains the greatest concentration of brown bears on earth, sometimes estimated at one per square mile.

Probably it was the Klondike gold rush of the 1890s that lured Hasselborg to Alaska from Minnesota, where he was born in 1876. He came via Mississippi and Florida. Like a lot of other young men he survived by mining, chopping plenty of wood, prospecting, salmon fishing, trapping, and guiding bear hunters from a base in Juneau. He visited the city only to buy salt and to check the general delivery mailbox for his infrequent mail. Eventually Hasselborg saved enough money to build a 30-foot boat on Douglas Island. It was sturdy enough to cope with raging storms, the

A fight erupted between these two grizzlies when they suddenly met in a river bottom. It ended just as suddenly when one retreated.

powerful tides, and often angry waters of southeast Alaska. He named the boat *Edda* after a sister. With it Hasselborg was able to range farther and farther,

hunting and fishing, living off the land. Brown bears of the Panhandle especially interested him.

A big break came in 1907 when Hasselborg, with his boat, was chartered by the Alexander Scientific Expedition of California, whose members were interested in geology and minerals, as well as the bears, and kelp and other sea life. Naturally curious and intelligent, the taciturn Hasselborg learned a lot about

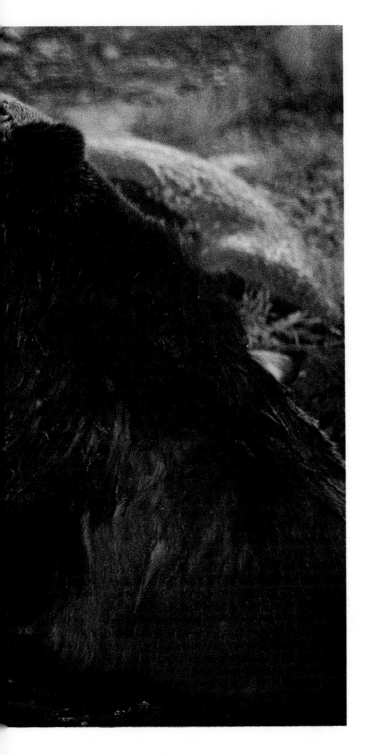

tures, for the Smithsonian Institution in Washington and other organizations. But experienced as he had become, he learned a bitter lesson one afternoon in 1912 at Bartlett Cove in Glacier Bay, where I was to land by seaplane over a half century later.

About 5 miles from his camp on shore, Hasselborg spotted the special bear he was seeking for a museum client in the East. Even from a distance it appeared to be a giant among browns. Stalking close, the animal proved to be even bigger than judged, and that fact may have caused the hunter only to wound the animal with two hasty shots. Even though darkness was falling, Hasselborg decided to track the bear and finish the job, a foolish mistake that a lot of hunters have made before and after him.

Maybe the bear actually waited in ambush for the tracker, but probably Hasselborg simply stumbled onto him in his haste or overconfidence. In any case the bear knocked him down, and bit and tore at his body. By playing dead and no doubt going into shock, Hasselborg apparently convinced the bear he *was* dead. Then the fatally wounded animal walked away.

There was no feeling in Hasselborg's shoulder, and later he recalled thinking he would lose that arm if not his life. He managed to drag himself to his feet and found the bear lying dead not far away. Half-dead himself and losing blood, Hasselborg stumbled to his skiff. Indians found him and helped him aboard his anchored boat. Then, alone, he cruised first to Hoonah, an Indian encampment, and on to Juneau. There, somehow, doctors managed to save his arm.

After a recovery of sorts, Hasselborg returned to Glacier Bay, retrieved the bear skull, and sent it to the museum that had ordered it. Undaunted by the mauling, he was soon hunting again.

Beginning almost as soon as the first Europeans waded ashore, wild Alaska has been a place for men to find escape, often in which to vanish, for a variety of reasons and for the rest of their lives. The Alaskan bush can get a solid grip on a man who relishes solitude and natural beauty, challenge, and peace. Long-bearded and 40 years old, Hasselborg went into virtual isolation on Admiralty Island, four years after his mauling, where for the remainder of his days he would be surrounded by bears. He built a one-room cabin with an adjacent root cellar and tool shed beside a river emptying into Mole Harbor. The only outsiders he saw, and these only occasionally, were the gun hunters he guided at first, and later the photographers and bear watchers. During the years at Mole Harbor, Hasselborg probably learned more about brown bears than anyone until that time.

As director of the old (before statehood) Alaska Game Commission, Frank Dufresne lived with bears,

scientific methods and record keeping as he cruised from Prince of Wales Island north to the Kenai. He encountered bears galore and kept logs of everything he saw. Word of his abilities soon spread, and for a while Hasselborg was kept busy collecting brown bear specimens for museums around the world.

Late in life Hasselborg admitted to having killed more than 200 bruins, among countless other crea-

A rich variety of seashore life, such as this hermit crab, occurs along the Pacific Coast. For a small sampling, walk the beaches and explore the tide pools during lowest tides.

off and on, for four decades. He knew Hasselborg about as well as anyone. "Allen had an uncanny sense about bears," Dufresne told me during a fishing trip in the 1960s to Hasselborg Lake, named after the hermit-bachelor. One day a visiting young cameraman followed a brown bear sow and her cub upstream in an attempt to get close-up pictures. The guide noted that the female bruin gave no sign whatever that she knew she was being followed. Therefore it was very puzzling to the photographer when he rounded a bend to find only an empty river up ahead.

According to Dufresne, the photographer started ahead again, but Hasselborg stopped him and probably saved his life. The mother had hustled her cub far out of sight in dense alders and then returned quietly to take care of her pursuer. She was crouched on her haunches no more than 15 yards away, behind a deadfall. Hasselborg spotted her licking her mouth, her jaws working and teeth showing. Calmly he managed to turn the cameraman back and away, fearing that if the eyes of the two met, the bruin would charge.

Later the pair sighted a large male bear walking on the trail ahead of them, and this one also glanced back without any apparent recognition. With the men following at a safe distance, the bear suddenly paused to scratch its back against a hemlock limb. Next it stood on hind feet and clawed away a patch of bark as high as it could reach. Dropping down again to all fours, the bear stared at the men for a moment before disappearing into dense timber.

Hasselborg pointed out the difference in the two bear behaviors. The sow had a cub to protect and was ready to do so. The male was more confident and laid back; a demonstration of his considerable size was sufficient.

Incidentally, that same big bear as well as others would come and rub their backs vigorously against Hasselborg's cabin, shaking up everything inside. This was especially alarming in the middle of the night. Although the old-timer was seriously injured on another occasion, the details remain unknown. He learned to deal with most of the Mole Harbor bears simply by standing his ground and talking to them. Apparently it always worked, or at least often enough.

After unaccountably selling his house and land in 1954, Hasselborg piloted his boat for the last time to Juneau, rode for the first time in a Ford auto, and boarded a plane (also for the first time) to fly to Florida to join his sister. But unable to stand the heat, the

A Tanner crab is just one of a tremendous variety
of sea creatures found along the southeast coast.

people, or the absence of his bears, he soon wrote to the Pioneer's Home in Sitka: "I want a place in your home but don't know how to apply."

The "grouchy" old man was accepted but wasn't able to endure the crowding—the "entrapment"—for very long. When Hasselborg died at 80 in 1956, a fascinating chapter in the history of southeast Alaska was closed.

During my most recent trip to Alaska on the Marine Highway, while cruising past Admiralty Island, I asked the U.S. Forest Service ranger-naturalist, who was then lecturing on board the M/V *Columbia*, about the fate of Allen Hasselborg's homestead. But unfortunately she had never heard of the bear man at all. She alleged that the lake and river were named after a defunct mining company.

ADMIRALTY ISLAND AND SOUTH. Most of Admiralty Island—921,000 acres of rolling spruce-hemlock forest interspersed with muskeg—is now secure within the Admiralty Island National Monument and Wilderness. The Tlingit Indian name of Xoots-noowu, fortress of bears, remains apt because the population of browns in 1987 still exceeded that of humans. An even greater number of Sitka blacktail

deer thrive on the island. Timberline is between 1,500 and 2,000 feet, where the forest gradually blends into alpine tundra with rock outcroppings and permanent snow and ice fields. Harbor seals, sea lions, and whales are common in the surrounding saltwater bays.

Among the great outdoor adventures possible in Southeast—in fact in all wild Alaska—is a cross-Admiralty canoe trip. Beginning at Mole Harbor (Hasselborg's homestead), experienced canoeists can strike out westward via a complex of lakes, rivers, and wilderness shelters to Angoon, an Indian community on the west side of the island, served by the Marine Highway. The scenic trip can be made in five days by very rugged and determined paddlers and portagers, but seven or eight days is a better target because the trout fishing and wildlife watching are superb along the way. Keep in mind that it is possible to carry canoes or kayaks to southeastern Alaska on the car ferries of the Marine Highway.

The two national forests of southeast Alaska, Tongass and Chugach (offices in Juneau, Petersburg, Sitka, Ketchikan, and Anchorage), maintain a system of 170 remote cabins, some located on Admiralty and other wilderness areas, that can be reserved at a cost of $10 per night. Since these places are in remote

Both pages: Scenes in southeastern Alaska are of incomparable beauty. There are
thousands miles of uninhabited coast to explore.

areas, the cost of getting there (usually by charter floatplane) can be the main expense. But their wilderness experience is hard to match.

Misty Fiords National Monument and Wilderness, 2,850,000 acres of raw wild land in extreme southeastern Alaska, contains the second largest designated wilderness in the United States. Remote parts of it have never known human footprints, and few areas contain so many wildlife species that require solitude and seclusion. These include trumpeter swans, wolverines, pine martens, and wolves. All five species of Alaskan salmon spawn in the Misty Fiords streams, often close to tidewater. If not for the often rainy weather and inaccessibility (by boat or charter floatplane only) which keeps it from being better known, this land of lava flows and glaciation might be re-

garded by everyone everywhere as among the scenic wonders of the world.

A similar place for adventurous people to explore is Tracy Arm-Ford's Terror between Petersburg and Juneau, up against the Canadian border. Here two fiords, Tracy and Endicott Arms, penetrate deep into the Alaska Coastal Range to create stunning scenery. Endicott was named for a crew member, Ford for a naval officer. These men in 1899 rowed from their ship into the narrow canyon at slack tide. There they were trapped in the surging, angry tidal current filled with icebergs for six terrifying hours until the tide finally changed. Ford's terror, to be sure.

Splendid and lovely as it is, even through the ocean mists, southeastern Alaska is only the beginning, the sea-level gateway to the rest of wild Alaska.

CHAPTER THREE
Denali National Park

I have never met a grizzly bear exactly like Frank. To rangers of Denali National Park during the summer of 1987, Frank was simply number 115, a blond grizzly, and an almost daily nuisance, if not exactly a menace. Peggy and I believe he was simply an extremely interesting wild animal. With affection, we gave him the name Frank—after two other Franks who are old friends of excellent character: Frank Craighead, the pioneer grizzly researcher of Yellowstone Park, and my valued friend Frank Sayers of Ostrander, Ohio. During countless hunting and fishing trips long ago, Frank Sayers taught me more about decency and the outdoors than any man before or since.

Strange as it may seem, the first time I saw Frank, the bruin, he was sedated and pictured on television. This occurred one evening in late June as I watched the local news in an Anchorage motel room. The day before, Frank had bitten an amateur photographer, Lee Grimstead of Wasilla, who had been trying to photograph him at close range. When Frank in turn approached, the photographer neither retreated nor shouted, nor tried to bluff the bear away. Instead he immediately rolled up in a ball on the ground, where he suffered tooth punctures in his calf before Frank walked away in search of other distractions. There seemed to be nothing really malicious in the act and the photographer was able to get up and make his way to the road not far away.

Very soon a bus from Denali's North Face Lodge came along, driven by Ken Carley. Fortunately, it would seem, one of the passengers was a Dutch doctor-psychiatrist on holiday, but the instant she saw the bloody Grimstead, who was then going into shock, she also went into shock. The victim was finally given first aid by workers at a Denali road maintenance camp and then flown to an Anchorage hospital where he

Mt. McKinley, in Denali National Park,
is the highest peak in North America.

quickly recovered with nothing more than an unhappy memory.

So Frank became locally famous, or infamous, depending on your viewpoint. He was easy to find and identify because of his light color and because he lived mostly in the Highway Pass sector. A party of park rangers promptly located and shot Frank with a tranquilizer dart for close examination. He was found to weigh only 140 pounds (or only about half of what most observers usually guessed). He was 3½ years old and in excellent health. In other words he had no physical problems that might make him mean. Most bears that bite people in parks are either eliminated or moved to an even more remote area, but Frank was given another chance after being fitted with a radio collar to keep track of his location thereafter. A metal tag with number 115 was clamped to one of his ears.

A week later, early on a clear morning, Peggy and I first found Frank grazing on the tender green grass just south of Highway Pass, and it was evident immediately that this was no ordinary bear. Most male grizzlies of interior Alaska seem to plod grimly through life, heads always down. They rarely do anything interesting from a photographer's standpoint. But not Frank. After grazing for a while he would jog a spell, then chase a ground squirrel or two before rolling over on his back to enjoy the glorious morning sunlight. He was a wonderful, compelling animal to watch.

The second day we saw Frank he was even busier. Earlier, also near Highway Pass, we had watched four wolves give unsuccessful chase to a pair of caribou bulls. After being easily outdistanced, the four retreated into a brushy draw where they disappeared. A few minutes later, as if on cue, from the opposite direction and toward the draw, Frank came along completely unaware of what lay before him. With our longest telephoto lenses focused on the spot, we waited tensely for something spectacular to happen.

Top are views of Frank, a grizzly whose antics and history made him one of the most compelling bears we've photographed. Above is the Arctic ground squirrel, Denali's principal prey of larger birds and many mammals, including Frank.

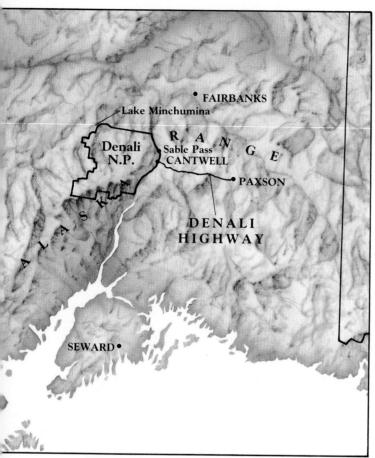

SELECTED SITES FROM THIS CHAPTER

We were somewhat disappointed. Suddenly the four wolves materialized out of the draw and made a short, snarling rush toward Frank, who gave the impression that he didn't even see them. This response seemed to confuse the wolves because seconds later all five were walking away in different directions, Frank having deviated not at all from his original path.

Because of the permafrost, the geology, and often the prolonged bad weather, the single, unpaved trans-park road is in need of frequent repair and maintenance. So graders and bulldozers are parked at intervals on unattended turnoffs, ready for immediate use. One afternoon Frank was digging into an undercut bank for ground squirrels, so far without success, when suddenly a ground squirrel darted out of its den to seek refuge in the iron innards of a D-7 bulldozer parked nearby. Frank followed right behind. Somehow in his single-minded pursuit, Frank found himself in the bulldozer cab where he made a shambles of the upholstery before finding his way outside again, still without his protein.

That same day a pair of hikers spotted Frank nearby. In a hasty attempt to quickly increase the distance between themselves and the now notorious bruin, they left their heavy packs behind. Of course Frank found the packs, nibbled around the edges of their foam mattress pads, and went exploring for something more interesting.

Forgive me for spending so much space on Frank and giving him human characteristics. But since my first trip to Denali (then Mt. McKinley National Park) in the 1950s, I have returned countless times, never failing to add a memorable experience or an unfor-

56

A lone grizzly stalks across still-snow-covered Toklat River bottom in Denali.

gettable creature to a now long list of them. Our encounters with Frank—very lucky encounters—are only the most recent.

DENALI—A BRIEF HISTORY. Denali is one of the four or five greatest big-game sanctuaries we have visited. Probably only the McNeil River State Game Sanctuary, also in Alaska, has gripped me as much or has thrilled me more. Denali is actually the heart of an immense wild area that sprawls across the center of the Alaska Range of mountains. The dominant topographic feature of Denali is Mt. McKinley, which towers nearly four vertical miles into the sky to 20,230 feet, the highest peak in North America. Many visitors come halfway around the world to see that white giant. Alone and on a bright day when visibility is good, McKinley is a stunning spectacle worth whatever the visitor has invested. But to me not even the Great One (the name the natives gave the peak long ago) matches in spectacle the wildlife that stalks this haunting wilderness.

Consider some statistics. Denali National Park and Preserve today protects for all time 6 million acres. That's a tract slightly larger than Massachusetts. Quite a large chunk of that is covered by glaciers and the massif of Mt. McKinley and Mt. Foraker, which are not wildlife habitat. The rest of the park contains an estimated 8,000 head of big game. Researchers report about 2,500 each of Dall or white sheep and barren-ground caribou, about 2,700 moose, 500 each of grizzly and black bears, and between 20 and 40 wolves at any one time. This is the only American national park where the white sheep and caribou may be seen. And it's the best park for a look at grizzlies. Denali's black bears are seldom noted. During my many visits, I have seen only two, one of these a very big one.

The officially estimated number of wolves puzzles me. I think it may be low. For many years I did not see a wolf at all, but recently they have become more and more evident. In 1986 we saw at least seven different wolves and in 1987 at least 11 during a short enough time period and over a great enough distance that we weren't counting any twice. Many of these were very close to the road. Of course wolves may finally be acclimatizing to the presence of increasing numbers of people. But more on Denali wolves later in this chapter.

We have no idea about the identity of the first nonnative to visit what is today Denali Park, or who was the first to see the landmark that is Mt. McKinley. The first published map ever to show the mountain probably was prepared by Baron Ferdinand von Wrangell and printed in 1839 in Leningrad by the Imperial Russian Academy of Sciences. Earlier maps by British captains James Cook and George Vancouver did not include the mountain.

The first American to explore the Denali region was William H. Dall, who with Frederick Whymper (brother of the first man to scale Europe's Matterhorn) traveled up the Yukon in a skin boat, or *bidarka*, to the Tanana junction. In 1878 Irish-born trapper-trader Arthur Harper came down the Tanana where he reported seeing "a great ice mountain just to the south." But as late as a century ago the general region of the park remained mostly a mystery until a U.S. Geological Survey team led by surveyors Robert Muldrow and George Eldridge (for whom glaciers were named) explored the area. They also plotted the general route

of the Alaska Railroad, which would be built 25 years later from Seward, on the ocean, past today's entrance to Denali National Park to Fairbanks. At about the same time the mountain was, for obscure reasons, named after Senator William McKinley of Ohio, subsequently to be elected 25th president of the United States. McKinley never saw the peak, nor did he ever visit Alaska. Nor did he care a whit about either.

The year 1906 brought a visitor to Denali who played the most important role in the eventual establishment of the park. Charles Sheldon was among the most serious and restless of American hunter-naturalists of that era. He was a strong and durable man who was also a keen observer and genuine lover of wilderness at a time when wilderness was considered only something to be overcome. Sheldon had two other great assets: money and influence in the eastern establishment. He resolved to explore the north side of the Alaska Range to study the habits of Dall sheep and other large animals, an undertaking many of his friends regarded as bizarre.

Early in the summer Sheldon left Fairbanks on the riverboat *Dusty Diamond* with a packer, Harry Karstens, and his five packhorses. The two men spent 45 days within present park boundaries, where they enjoyed unequaled opportunities to study wild species, large and small. They walked in lonely wilderness where few natives and fewer, if any, nonnatives had wandered before. The experience was so mystical for Sheldon that he resolved to return and spend an entire winter.

In August 1907, Sheldon returned with Karstens and remained almost a full year, leaving millions of footprints on the mountainsides and in the river bottoms. His diary frequently mentions his hope that this wild scenic treasure be set aside as a national park.

Once back in New York and Washington, DC, where all power resided, Sheldon swung into action. As chairman of the game committee of the influential Boone & Crockett Club, he convinced that group that they must endorse a system of game refuges for wild Alaska, especially for the Mt. McKinley area. It was the first time anyone had ever proposed such a grand undertaking. Sheldon also drummed away at the U.S. Biological Survey (today the U.S. Fish & Wildlife Service), at Stephen Mather (director of the fledgling National Park Service), at Alaska's territorial delegate to Congress, James Wickersham (who had once tried to climb McKinley), even at builders of the Alaska Railroad, to help save the Denali area as a people's national park.

In 1917 the persistence and pressure paid off. Both houses of Congress finally agreed on a bill. And Pres-

Denali is the best place in which to look for Dall sheep. The rams are most accessible in spring and early summer, when they are at lower elevations.

tions, and a road maintenance complex. Only the first 18 miles of the road are paved. This hardtopped section opens in mid-May (the rest later as snow removal and weather permit) and remains open until closed by snow in early fall. The unpaved portion becomes very dusty during dry periods and sloppy in rain. But once beyond the sight and sounds of the road, either north or south, there remains to this day raw wilderness with only faint game trails.

WILDLIFE AND NATURALISTS OF DENALI.

A good many naturalists and environmentalists have made pilgrimages or studied at Denali over the years. Fortunately I met one of these men on my first trip. I wanted to photograph Dall sheep rams on an assignment for *Outdoor Life* magazine but, despite days of hard, steep hiking, was having a difficult time finding them. So I stopped by the small log cabin ranger station at Igloo Creek to seek advice. There I met biologist Adolph Murie, brother of well-known biologist Olaus Murie, who knew the sheep of Denali, as well as the wolves that sometimes preyed on them, better than anyone. Murie not only told me where to locate my rams, but on subsequent afternoons when it was dreary and raining outside he revealed more about his fascinating life and research in the sanctuary.

Altogether Adolph Murie spent 25 summers in Denali from 1922, when it was roadless, to 1970, which gave him a picture of the natural history no other observer could match. During the late 1930s there appeared to be a dangerous dip in the population of white sheep, immediately blamed on too many wolves. One of Murie's goals was to examine the "serious" situation. So from 1939 through 1941 he concentrated on the wolf–sheep relationship. In his report *The Wolves of Mt. McKinley* (1944), he concluded that wolf predation certainly existed and had a beneficial effect on sheep; that the two were in equilibrium as they had been for countless centuries. In fact the two species had evolved together there in the wild Alaska Range.

Murie preferred wildlife biology study by serious, accurate, prolonged observation in the field, rather than by some of the newer techniques just coming into common use, such as live capture and collaring. He was interested in everything: haymice, or singing voles, which dry and store vegetation for winter use. The wandering tattler, an elusive shorebird. Lemmings. Lynxes. Wolverines. But it always seemed to me that his enthusiasm increased noticeably when discussing grizzly bears. That's easy enough to understand.

One day during the 1960s, after spending a long

ident Woodrow Wilson signed the document, carried to him personally by Charles Sheldon, preserving four million acres. The old sourdough and packer Harry Karstens became the first park superintendent. In 1980, during the environmentally concerned administration of President Jimmy Carter, the original park area was increased by about 50 percent to its present 6-million-acre size.

What is so remarkable, so pleasing to report, is that Denali remains largely as wild and unspoiled as Charles Sheldon found it. The single major alteration by man is the one and only park road. It was begun in 1922 and by 1930 ran westward from the park entrance (on Alaska Route 3, the Parks Highway) to Wonder Lake. In the end it stretched a total of 88 miles to a mining boom town, now largely a ghost town, in the green Kantishna Hills. The road makes it possible to pass through an absolute wilderness by motor vehicle on one of the world's final frontiers. The only other human developments within Denali are six campgrounds, a midpark visitor center, simple ranger sta-

summer day photographing sheep, I was hiking on a mountain overlooking the Toklat River when I spotted a grizzly at about the same time it saw or heard me. Grazing, it suddenly looked up at me. I kept moving at the same pace, resisting the urge to walk more quickly down a brushy slope toward the park road, even though the bruin now came laterally toward my path of descent as if to intercept me. When it sniffed where I had passed, the bear turned and followed me. I guarantee that it is eerie to have a silvertip tracking you. But still I didn't hurry, which proved best. After staying on my trail for 100 yards or so, the bear abruptly stopped and began grazing again. The next time that it was raining too hard to carry cameras into the field, I told Murie about the experience. He affirmed that that silvertip's behavior wasn't unusual and chuckled, as I recall, adding that no grizzly behavior was really unusual.

Very early one summer, again while stalking sheep with a camera on Primrose Mountain, I saw a bear digging furiously on a slope well below me. At first I thought it was pursuing ground squirrels, but then it walked a short distance away and, from a clump of brush, dragged the carcass of a bull caribou into the fresh excavation. The bruin next covered it by scraping soil with forepaws and finally lay down, legs outstretched, practically on top of the mound. At the time this burial seemed to me very strange behavior. But I soon learned that grizzlies commonly bury carrion, no matter how they obtain it. I also learned to be much more alert and observant when hiking the Denali backcountry, especially in spring when more carrion from winter kills is available. It is a mistake ever to approach a grizzly bear food cache because grizzlies guard over them, often unseen.

The supply of carrion varies from spring to spring, depending on the severity of the winter just past. But some moose, caribou, and sheep are certain to die or are killed. Unless the carcasses are quickly covered with snow, they are devoured by creatures that do not hibernate, such as wolverines, foxes, ravens, and Canada jays. Soon after coming out of their long winter sleep, bears eat ravenously any carrion they come across and then cache what is left. It makes no difference if a caribou died of disease months before, or, if weakened, was recently killed by a wolf; the first bear to come along will claim it. A larger bear might arrive to drive off a smaller one.

Just east of Denali Park during the winter of 1962–63, a number of caribou were covered by a snow avalanche on a mountain slope near Denali Lake. That bonanza of bodies kept at least seven grizzlies in the immediate area, feeding throughout most of the following summer. As the season advanced and more snow melted, more carcasses were uncovered to provide a continuing feast for the bears.

Charles Sheldon often related an incident of food caching he saw on his trip of discovery in 1906. Somehow seven Dall rams had been killed, maybe also by an avalanche. A grizzly sow with three cubs found one of them. She seized the carcass in her jaws, dragged it into a hollow, and covered it so well with rocks that it was barely visible. She then climbed farther up the mountainside to another carcass and buried it in a similar manner. The cubs following her became increasingly curious and excited all the time.

As the female left the second carcass, one cub discovered that the meat was palatable. It pawed away some of the rocks and began to eat. When the mother saw this, she rushed back and cuffed the cub hard enough to make it bawl and run away. After covering the sheep again, she started away, this time closely followed by all three contrite cubs. But suddenly the sow grizzly ran back, as if to reassure herself that the

Wolverines, like bears, obtain a goodly portion of their annual meat in spring from the hulks of winter-killed moose, caribou, and sheep.

Bull moose of Denali are most active and easily observed from the end of August onward. Coming into the rut then, this bull of Igloo Flat has just shed its velvet. The antlers remain bright red for several days afterward.

meat cache was not being disturbed. Fourteen times during about 20 minutes, according to Sheldon, the sow returned to check on the carcass, before settling down to nap in willows nearby. Later Sheldon saw her feeding on a third sheep carcass she had previously cached nearby on the slope. He watched her drag still another sheep 300 or 400 yards before hiding it, too.

Adolph Murie told me about watching another female with a 2-year-old cub uncover a cache of sheep. For a long time the 150-pound mother fed while the cub nibbled timidly at one edge. When the mother could hold no more, she pawed a little more debris over the carcass and collapsed right on top of it. Finally she rolled over and allowed the cub to nurse while she seemed asleep.

Although they do eat meat, the grizzlies subsist mostly on plant foods. And of the meat they do consume, not all is carrion. In Denali Park, grizzlies *seem* to have become adept at catching and killing young caribou and moose, especially the latter. At least park visitors nowadays are seeing more and more bear–moose interaction, particularly early in the season and sometimes quite near to park headquarters. In 1986

Peggy and I came across a straw-colored sow accompanied by a yearling cub. She had just killed a month-old moose calf near Savage River and had dragged it into dense willows to feed. Not much but bones and skin was left to be covered up after the first feeding.

A little later and about a mile away, we came upon a lone cow moose that had wounds on its rump and forelegs where big patches of hide had been torn away. We wondered if this was the mother of the calf just consumed.

Adolph Murie related another dramatic incident to me. One November, near Savage River, he located a bull moose of trophy dimensions. He estimated the antler spread at nearly 6 feet. When retrieved later on, the antlers weighed 50 pounds, confirming his assessment. From its unsteady stance and the saliva drooling from its mouth, Murie could see that the animal was in poor condition. On closer inspection, the naturalist realized that its face was badly scarred, and the white opacity in the eyes revealed that it had been blinded, probably in a rutting battle. Here was a huge wilderness monarch once a match for any grizzly or pack of wolves, now making a last stand in dark-

ness. Murie watched the bull for several days, during which time it dropped one antler, which he photographed. When the second fell, Murie weighed both.

Remarkably, the tenacious old bull moose was still alive in mid-January, two months after Murie had first found it. But on a bitter day in February, with the mercury at −20° F, a park ranger found its frozen carcass being covered by falling snow.

During the next month or so a wolverine, a fox, numerous ravens, and at intervals a black wolf gnawed at the exposed parts of the dead moose. If not frozen, the meat would have vanished quickly. But exceedingly low temperatures, packed snow, and circumstance saved much of that old monarch for the first groggy grizzly to leave its Denali den and find it about the middle of April.

Anyone interested in reading much more about Denali bears should obtain a copy of Adolph Murie's *The Grizzlies of Mount McKinley*, published by the University of Washington Press, Seattle. Scientists today generally agree that a single species of brown/grizzly bears, *Ursus arctos*, inhabits North America and Eurasia. The grizzly of Denali we have been discussing here is of the subspecies, *U. a. horribilis*.

To recall our golden days in Denali National Park is to begin a great flood of memories about different wild creatures that have enriched our days there. I naturally think about the lynx that long ago was almost a permanent resident of the Riley Creek campground, feeding on the fat parka squirrels there. I have not seen nearly enough wolverines in my wanderings, but one I saw at closest range was on Sable Pass at daybreak, where a visitor is more likely to meet grizzly bears. This one, as are most, was engrossed in traveling from horizon to horizon at a pace that seemed to burn up vast amounts of calories and protein.

Some summers we have seen a lot of red foxes and at other times only a few, if any at all. Today photography near or around a den is not permitted in Denali, but when it was, a day spent near such a site could be extremely exciting as well as a window onto their lifestyle. In one day at a den with a view overlooking the Toklat River, I saw adult foxes return with the following prey to feed three kits: arctic ground squirrels (all young), a tundra vole, two young magpies (probably just out of the nest), and a bird that was probably a golden plover.

Unless one or more kits failed to appear above-ground during my vigil, there were three kits in this fox family. Of the three, one was by far the boldest, and I wondered if this was a trait that would serve it well when finally grown. Not only was that bold kit the first to sniff and shake any new creature deposited at the den entrance by its parents, but it was also the one that showed great curiosity about me. On still unsteady legs, it would walk up to my tripod base, stare at me for a moment, then run back to the den, often only to repeat the process. Would this particular young fox have better odds for long-time survival than those that were much more shy? Or vice versa?

I learned much later that this fox den had originally been excavated by a grizzly bear. The summer, temporary ranger that reported this to me did not know if the growing kits were still in the den at the time, or if the site had been abandoned. But another fox family used the same site the following summer.

CARIBOU OF DENALI. The caribou of the park, which now exist in only a fraction of the numbers of, say, 1960 are the strangest and most unpredictable subjects for photographers. In May and early June, these circumpolar deer move from Lake Minchumina, northwest of Denali where most have wintered, eastward toward the Sanctuary and Teklanika river drainages. Now the herds are small, from a few animals to 50 or so, and these are not particularly attractive. With long hair faded and frayed, they are shedding winter coats at the same time they are finding new green plants—mostly sedge—to eat for a fresh lease on life. The terrible hardships of winter are past.

The warble and nostril flies that plague caribou throughout the summer cause almost continual annoyance. They may contribute most to the caribou's often strange, erratic behavior. Time and again I have had caribou seem to flee immediately at our sight, only to turn abruptly and come running right back, eventually to pose for pictures closer than my telephoto lens will accommodate. A young bull once came within 15 feet of me before pausing to stare in wild-eyed disbelief. I've also seen herds of caribou clustered close together on the only lingering patches of snow or ice on an entire green mountainside, maybe as some refuge or relief from mosquitos and warble flies.

Warbles lay eggs on hair of caribou legs and bellies. On hatching the larvae penetrate hair and hide, then travel to the saddle area where they emerge swollen in the spring. The living larvae of nostril flies are deposited in caribou noses, eventually to lodge en masse in the throat. The following spring they are coughed out to pupate on the tundra and mature as the terrible parasitic flies that torment caribou into their seemingly ridiculous behavior.

I took this shot of a young red fox before Denali's ban on photography near den sites. Intrusive people can greatly disturb fox parents.

In the flats below Polychrome Pass, this bull caribou with antlers in velvet grazes on
willow tips while keeping a wary eye on the photographer.

Flies are most active on clear, bright days, and this explains why we then look for most animals to be on higher, windier ridges, even snowfields, as they try to escape the attacks. Individual caribou may race about in panic to escape one fly, only to stop suddenly. I've seen many, after long zigzag running, stop and stand motionless for long periods, probably to escape detection and attack by their tormentors.

Few mammals anywhere are more handsome, more regal than the bulls of early autumn. By late August the magnificent antlers have hardened, and the velvet has peeled away to expose beams that at first are carmine from the film of blood left behind. Later the antlers lose the red color, but are especially noteworthy because caribou have the largest set of antlers of any of the deer family for their size. The annual rut is not far in the future.

Once on an eerie, foggy morning near Wonder Lake I saw two bulls approaching a creek mouth on a collision course. They were using the same game trail. Without hesitation, posturing, or any preliminaries, they went head to head, each trying to drive the other

back. This particular clash, though noisy, did not last long. After a minute or two, one acceded and both evaporated into low clouds on the same path, traveling in the same direction.

Yet, a little later, when the most powerful bulls would be vigilantly gathering and guarding harems of cows, any meeting of males might be much more violent. Serious injuries might be sustained. Charlie Ott, a pioneer cameraman who photographed the wildlife of Denali National Park longer than anyone else, told me that he once saw a magnificent white-maned bull lift an equally heavy caribou completely off its feet and then proceed to destroy it by repeated antler thrusts to the flank.

In the part of Denali Park known to tourists, the caribou herds do not spend the winter or even remain long after aspen and willow leaves fall. Single calves are born in May far from the park. Their coordination and speed develop so quickly they are soon able to accompany the herds in their long migrations. The calves that cannot keep up are those most likely to fall prey to wolves. Although, as elsewhere in the

North, wolves account for a good part of each spring's calf loss, a close relationship between the two species has existed for thousands of years. This is a clear case of survival of the fittest of both caribou and wolves.

During the year of my first visit to Denali only about 2,500 of the hardiest travelers came to the park, then accessible only by the Alaska Railroad or via the Denali Highway (today Alaska Route 8 from Paxson to Cantwell), which then was so rough that passage was often hardly possible. By 1987 visitation had increased almost 200-fold to about half a million. In recent years officials have found it necessary to prohibit private vehicle use on the single transpark road for most of its length beyond Savage River campground. The road simply cannot withstand the increasing ravages of so many cars. That leaves a choice today between the free, frequent, all-day-long shuttle buses provided by the park, and the more luxurious commercial tour buses. Passengers are free to get on and off the shuttle buses anywhere they like, except near grizzlies. Either way, riders are able to see a corner of wild Alaska, and its wild creatures, that would otherwise be impossible.

DALLS OF DENALI. Although I'm convinced most of the big game has become tolerant of the steady bus traffic, recent studies have shown that some animals are staying farther away from the highway. I believe this is most true of the white sheep that first attracted Charles Sheldon to the area.

During my early visits, Dall rams especially were much more visible on mountains close to the road than they are in summer now. Then it was fairly easy to spot the all-white animals on dark slopes and then climb close enough for photography. Wary and suspicious elsewhere, the Dalls of Denali were never fearful of photographers who approached them slowly while keeping a reasonable distance away. But memory can become unreliable, especially with age, so I checked my notes of Denali trips past for corroboration. I found that more sheep certainly were visible during the 1960s and 1970s. During a two-week period of July 1987, Peggy and I did not see any rams. It's not that they have vanished or fallen prey to wolves. I'm convinced they are simply keeping their distance from the traffic.

Most Denali sheep spend winters north of the road because strong winds blow exposed ridges free of snow, which is relatively light there anyway. Some remain on this winter range all year, but Adolph Murie was always intrigued by the way many, and perhaps most, migrated in May and June to headwaters far to the south. To do so the animals had to cross at least 2 miles, usually more, of unfamiliar low country where wolves and grizzlies were fairly numerous.

Murie believed the sheep were fully aware of their vulnerability when making the annual trek back and forth. The keen naturalist watched them spend a few days on departure ridges, carefully scrutinizing the terrain below, before making the break toward greener pastures, which included crossing the park road. Murie told me about bands of 60 or 70 ewes and lambs moving slowly across the lowlands in a compact group, but breaking into a gallop the instant any one of the older females sensed danger. Once on the high summering range, Murie noted that the sheep sometimes gamboled in play, as though the tension of the dangerous trip had been lifted. Most of the flock returned to original winter areas in August or September.

One summer Peggy and I found a group of ewes with lambs on Tattler Creek just east of Sable Pass. These animals had not, or not yet, made a southward migration. Tattler drains an exquisite area carpeted with wildflowers and also provides a passage for wandering wildlife. I once watched a wolverine unsuccessfully excavate for ground squirrels up Tattler Creek. And on rockslides pikas, tiny rock rabbits, protested when I sat too near their curing piles of "hay" while I watched and photographed the sheep, which were soaking up the sunny warmth of the short summer.

Dall lambs are especially appealing when you can observe them at close range. They seem less inclined than their mothers to waste July days bedded down and dozing. The two-month-old lambs were much more surefooted than they at first appeared. Peggy and I watched them cavort with one another, butting heads, and running in circles, before returning to their mothers and climbing on top of them or trying to nurse. After a short time these lambs on Tattler Creek slopes did not seem to have any fear of our presence among them. They may have been following the example of calm mothers that were quite habituated to finding people in that area. On one occasion a ewe stood up where she had been bedded down some distance away, stretched, walked in our direction, and lay down again about 30 feet away, *with her back toward us.* Only the ewe's ears revealed that she was aware of our slightest movement.

But like all wild sheep, Dalls depend on their sharp eyes rather than their hearing to detect danger. They have good noses too, but they cannot entirely depend on them because air currents at high elevations can carry confusing information. I have never seen sheep bed down where they did not have a strategic view of a large area below them.

As I was changing rolls of film in a camera, the ewe just below me suddenly stood up, alert. At first I thought she was disturbed by the metallic sounds of the camera, but she never looked back in my direction. Instead she directed her attention to something far below on the waterway. I had to search a long time and through binoculars before I finally saw a pair of young caribou bulls coming into view, following a game trail parallel to the stream. With sentinels like this, predators would find it almost impossible to creep up within attack range of the sheep.

Predators are not solely responsible for the great fluctuations in Denali's sheep numbers. The population has soared as high as 5,000 and hit an all-time low of about 500 in 1945. Deep snow and ice crust conditions are the elements that can make predation unusually easy. The oldest, youngest, and otherwise least able are the individuals first taken. The toughest, most tenacious, survive to breed future generations.

Dall rams particularly have immense esthetic appeal, largely because their haunts are the most precipitous alpine ledge country at the top of wild Alaska. After a climb or hike over landscapes of forget-me-nots and spring beauties, of saxifrage and yellow Arctic poppies, my spirit grows strong and soars, although I may be weak in the knees from the exertion. At those same elevations in Alaska, I can be on a level with soaring golden eagles and gyrfalcons, as well as snow buntings and rosy finches. I see wheateaters that have flown all the way from Asia and surfbirds that have deserted their ocean beaches to nest on Denali ridges. I hope I never grow so infirm that I cannot climb and explore in cool, wild sheep country.

DENALI MOOSE. The world's largest deer, moose on the other hand thrive in the lowest elevations of Denali National Park. To me their northern coniferous forest habitat does not match the majesty of

Left: I hope I never grow so old or infirm that I cannot climb and explore in cool, wild sheep country. There, though weak in the knees from exertion, I am on a level with soaring golden eagles and gyrfalcons. Above: Larger bull moose of Denali range from 1200 to 1500 pounds, the largest sets of antlers spreading nearly 6 feet and weighing about 50 pounds. Moose usually stick to lower elevations.

By driving very early in the morning, when the traffic is thinnest, or late in the afternoon, you increase your odds of seeing moose, like this bull browsing on willow.

sheep range, but the animals themselves are highly impressive.

Often described as the archetypical mammals of the Ice Age, moose have massive bodies that store energy and hold heat during severest winters. In Denali they feed through long, subarctic days on willows unshaded by other trees. The willows grow in mineral-rich moist soils carried to moose habitat by glacial rivers. The end result is that the great mammals are the world's most powerful as well as largest deer. Charles Sheldon regarded moose as "a most noble form of wild life."

Some of the bulls of Igloo Creek, or of Savage and Sanctuary rivers, weigh from 1,200 to 1,500 pounds and stand 7 feet tall at the muscular shoulders. A few grow great palmate antlers almost 7 feet wide that weigh as much as 70 pounds.

We have enjoyed both rich experiences and surprises with Denali moose. Among the surprises was finding a bull at daybreak one morning atop Polychrome Pass, far above its normal environment. The animal walked along a cliff edge for a distance, as if to see the multicolored hills beyond the Toklat River forks in the distance, before descending into a deep draw where only sheep would usually tread.

Among the rich experiences were several evenings spent where a cold, transparent brook empties into the west end of Wonder Lake. The bay there is shallow enough that aquatic vegetation can grow and attract moose. Especially cows with spring calves come to feed here. Near dusk, Mt. McKinley rises in the background to create a classic scene of exquisite Alaskan wilderness. I would return to Denali any time just to pass summer evenings beside this bay of Wonder Lake.

Less serene were the times at Igloo Flats, where we watched the fall rut of Denali bull moose. Whereas Wonder Lake is cool blue, Igloo in early September is yellow with foliage of aspen and willow. In this low, level area black bulls with recently hardened scarlet antlers come in misty mornings searching and sniffing for the scent of female moose in estrus. On meeting, bulls begin the posturing and dueling process, studying and measuring and testing their rivals, to determine which are strongest and therefore which will do most of the fall's breeding.

Many bull-moose clashes are simply noisy, red-eyed shoving matches, sometimes in the open where photographers can shoot them, or half hidden in stands

From Polychrome Pass on a summer's day, and using a spotting scope, you can usually locate dozens of caribou and a grizzly bear or two.

of dark green spruce. If the day is dark (as too many are during the Denali autumn), the bulls come out in the open to settle the question of dominance. A really serious bull-moose contest can make anyone's pulse pound.

One September dawn when the whole of Igloo Flats was colored red and gold, muted with a thin crust of frost, I was maneuvering into position to photograph a heavy, grunting bull. Then another suddenly emerged from behind and seemed to catch my subject and me by surprise. The two lunged at each other, eyes rolling to show scarlet edges, and disappeared into a thicket where I had no business following. For several minutes the sounds of combat, the crashing antlers, the snapping limbs, and the crunch of undergrowth must have been audible a mile away. Later, when the arena was quiet again, I saw my original subject limping badly on its left foreleg. For him, the rutting season was off to an unpromising start.

A WOLF–MOOSE ENCOUNTER. Except at Riley Creek, the park entrance, the public campgrounds of Denali are fairly small, and the wilderness atmosphere is not too greatly diminished. There are individual camping spaces, faucets with pure running water until late August (when pipes begin to freeze), several outhouses, a community bear-proof food cache, and nothing more. No electricity. No flush toilets. Whenever there is space available, Peggy and I opt for Teklanika campground where we have spent, altogether, more than a hundred nights in everything from a confined nylon mountain tent and the bare bed of a pickup truck to, most recently, a VW camper van. That last is a concession to entering the Social Security age, which also gives a 50 percent discount on the camping fee. Our preference for Teklanika proved especially fortunate in July 1987 when we left the campground soon after daybreak and traveled westward along the Teklanika River.

Beginning not far from camp limits, road travel offers glimpses through the trees of the braided, almost half-mile-wide, glacial waterway. We always watch it

The East Fork River (left) has braided channels that typify many glacial waterways. These channels are used by wildlife for travel and protection, as evidenced in the photo sequence beginning above on the Teklanika River. Here a young bull moose seeks protection in fast deep water from a lone wolf. The ensuing drama shown on upcoming pages spanned two full days and ended under difficult photo conditions.

closely because grizzlies frequently commute along the river. But this morning Peggy said suddenly, "Stop. I just saw a moose—running."

A moment later she added that a wolf was chasing the moose. We parked, affixed cameras to tripods, and hurried through dense alders toward the river. Thirty-six hours would pass before, exhausted, we saw our Teklanika campsite again.

After negotiating the dense strip of trees and brush that separated the road from the river, we came upon a grim scene. A yearling bull moose with short, spike antlers was standing unsteadily in the nearest, murky glacial-melt channel of the Teklanika River, gulping great amounts of the ice-cold water. Its left rear leg was ripped and bloody, and appeared useless. While the yearling stood at bay, leaning into the force of the current, a single pale gray wolf sat watching it intently from the opposite bank. As we set up tripods not far away, the wolf stretched out, half dozing in the weak morning sunshine. Even when the moose limped out onto the near river bank and stood there, the wolf only glanced up, then dozed again. It seemed to know that a successful outcome for him was only a matter of time and patience.

During that whole day, throughout the early July night that never got completely dark, and through the second day, the wolf made 14 different attacks on the moose within a stretch of about 400 yards of riverbed. Time and again after long periods, often after hours of inactivity, the wolf rushed its prey and usually managed to get a grip on a leg, the underbelly, a flank, and at least once on the nose, and tried to drag the moose down. But each time the yearling bull would manage to reach swift, deeper water where the wolf could not maintain either a foothold or its jaw-hold and was washed downstream, forced to break off the encounter. Two or three times the moose managed weak counterattacks, striking at its tormentor with front hooves. The wolf appeared to favor one foot from the beginning but afterward seemed to move with a more definite limp.

During the long twilight and predawn, the life-and-death drama continued in slow motion. Between attacks the moose and wolf would lie on opposite banks of the river channel facing one another, the moose often gulping water while lying down at river's edge. All the while Peggy and I wondered when more wolves

Continued from previous page: The young bull was gulping great amounts of water. Its left rear leg was ripped and bloody, and appeared useless . . . The wolf stretched out, half dozing in the weak morning sunshine. (Sequence continues)

Continued from previous pages: Over two days the wolf made 14 different attacks
covering about 400 yards of river. But each time the young bull managed to reach
deep swift water where the wolf could not maintain foothold or jaw-hold. Late in the
second evening, the drama ended. (See text for details.)

or a grizzly bear would come along and put a sudden end to it. During summer, wolves tend to hunt alone more often than in groups. But by sunrise the moose was still clinging to life and once again dragged the wolf into wild water where the moose tried to trample it.

All the while we were trying to photograph the struggle, too often from a great distance and usually through scattered openings in the vegetation. About 24 hours after Peggy had first spotted the moose, rain began to fall. Soaked ourselves, we had to keep cameras and lenses covered in heavy plastic trash bags. More than once we discussed giving up the vigil, but wolf attacks on large prey in full view of people take place too seldom to be missed.

Late on the second evening in gloom and a steady cold drizzle, the young bull fell. It seemed to crumple into the water's edge and could not get on its feet again. Almost leisurely the wolf climbed onto it and began tearing at the carcass. Both were caught in the powerful current and together drifted out of sight downstream. Not much later and thoroughly exhausted, Peggy and I crawled into a warm, dry sleeping bag.

Later we learned more about the protagonists in what might to some people seemed a cruel killing. According to Tom Meier, a biologist of the Denali Wolf Research Project, the predator was a male and probably the A or alpha male of what is known as the East Fork–Toklat pack. From year to year this

longtime resident pack contains from 6 to 13 wolves, usually about 8. At the time of the attack, the pack contained five new pups in a den not far away. The East Fork–Toklat pack is regarded by biologists as the only one that ranges entirely within Denali Park and perhaps the only pack in Alaska not subject to hunting or trapping over some part of its range.

In April 1986 the alpha male had been darted by helicopter and live-captured. It was judged to be five or six years old and even then, with a full stomach, it weighed only 105 pounds, or considerably less than adult gray wolves are believed to average. Its right ear was sliced in half, a result of some old injury. It was also missing an outside toe on the front left foot, which may account for the limp we saw.

A biologist team from the Wolf Project was able to locate the carcass of the moose some distance down the Teklanika River from where it had succumbed. On examination, they estimated its body weight at about 350 pounds, less than that of a normal yearling male in July, and its bone marrow content showed it to be in generally poor condition. If the moose had been healthy it probably would not have become the victim of a single wolf, which may have instinctively recognized easy prey.

During our busy summer of 1987 in wild Alaska, Peggy and I saw many extraordinary sights and creatures. Frank, the blond grizzly bear, for example. But nothing quite matched the stark, savage encounter of moose and wolf along the Teklanika River.

Speaking of Frank, grizzly number 115, we got further news of him. Although often seen throughout the summer of 1987 and until late September when the park road was closed, he had no further encounters with people. Almost surely he went into hibernation in a winter den somewhere within Denali's borders. We hope to see Frank again.

CHAPTER FOUR
Katmai and Other Parks

On a cool gray morning in summer 1966, Toni Peterson stepped outside her cabin to hang up laundry. Nothing unusual there, except that the cabin was really a wilderness fishing camp situated beside the narrow channel that connects Grosvenor Lake with Colville Lake in Katmai National Park, then a National Monument. Toni was alone at the time, and her nearest neighbors were at park headquarters on the Brooks River, about 40 miles away as the raven flies. A faulty transmitter had left her without even radio contact with anyone.

Before her chore was finished, Toni had a strange, sinking perception that she was not alone. And she wasn't. From the corner of her eye she noticed a movement in the brush near the cabin. She turned and found herself facing a large whitish wolf. The animal, its head held low, stood little more than 30 feet away, regarding her through cold yellow eyes.

Toni Peterson remembers being suddenly liquid in the knees but managing to hurry toward the open cabin door. There, almost barring the way, stood another, darker wolf. Somehow she made it inside and instantly slammed the door and bolted it. Then she sat down, too faint to stand.

There is no logical explanation for what followed because it is not normal wolf behavior. All that day and throughout the next, the two wolves remained within sight of the cabin. At intervals during the night they howled and were answered by other wolves across the narrows. It was a chilling, primeval counterpoint.

Although she later realized she had been foolish, Toni remained a prisoner in her cabin for several days. She had heard all the usual stories about savage, bloodthirsty wolves. But eventually, after the animals appeared far more curious than aggressive, she opened the door a crack and tossed out leftover pancakes, bacon, and fish, hoping they would take the food and go away. The wolves approached cautiously and gob-

Above: For several weeks, wolves frequented the area of a fishing camp on Grosvenor Lake. Previous page: From the air the cratered surface of Katmai National Park is a scene of total wilderness, cold and beautiful.

bled the handouts, but of course instead of leaving they sat down as if awaiting more.

To pass the time, Toni made up another batch of sourdough cakes, and the wolves ate these, too. Gradually the woman regained her courage, even stepping just outside the door. When the wolves seemed indifferent, she even retrieved the laundry that had spent several days on the line. Gradually she returned to a normal routine, while the wolves simply watched her or followed at a distance like a pair of family dogs.

I might not have believed this account if the two wolves had not been sitting at water's edge when I arrived by floatplane with Johnny Walatka to spend a few days fishing there in 1966. In fact I was often able to photograph the pair and caught fleeting glimpses of others. There seemed to be seven or eight

While we casted for trout one evening at Katmai's Grosvenor Lake, a pair of wolves watched us from the shore.

in the pack, but none of the others were so bold. I learned later that the original two wolves remained in the Grosvenor-Colville cabin area for about a month after I left, then disappeared as mysteriously as they had arrived. They may have been among the same group I met a year later about 15 miles away on the American River, a salmon spawning stream that drains into the opposite end of Coville Lake just outside Katmai Park.

But no matter, the incident that was part of my introduction to beautiful Katmai will remain vivid as long as I live.

THE KATMAI REGION. We have almost no written record or description of the Katmai region before the momentous earthquakes of 1912. Eskimos and their ancestors are known to have hunted and fished there since about 2400 B.C., and it is believed they moved out of their wood and earthen dwellings during some fearful period of geological instability. Then, in June 1912, a series of violent earthquakes rocked the land for five or six straight days. Suddenly the mountain between the ancient villages of Katmai and Sa-

vonoski, called Novarupta today, exploded with a force modern scientists regard as among the two or three most powerful in world history.

Masses of rock and pumice vaulted so high from the throat of the volcano that crews of Russian vessels over 50 miles away in Shelikof Strait could see it. White ash then began to stream from the main vent and also from nearby fissures. Within minutes 2½ cubic miles of ash were expelled, and sweeping down the adjacent valley came a flow of incandescent sand. Trees growing on slopes above the mass were snapped off and carbonized by a scorching wind. In the end more than 40 square miles of valley floor were buried as deep as 700 feet beneath the fine, pale dust.

When the particles that darkened the sky fell on the Russian ships, turning daylight into dusk, the seamen aboard thought they were witnessing the Apocalypse. The particles would eventually carry as far south as Seattle and San Francisco. A letter written by a young officer to his family reported that he would never see them again but would "think of them always from Paradise."

At about the same time Novarupta was belching

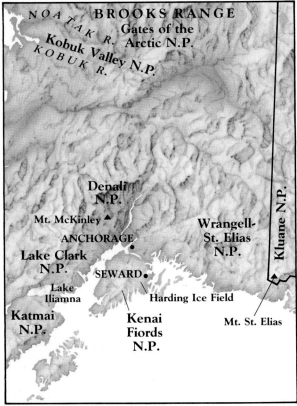

SELECTED SITES FROM THIS CHAPTER

destruction, another volcano, called Mount Katmai, 6 miles to the east, collapsed. In minutes the giant peak became a chasm, a hollow in the earth, 3 miles long by 2 miles wide. Vulcanologists believe that during the short space of 60 hours at least 7 cubic miles of volcanic substance was shot into the atmosphere, even to the stratosphere. The material fell to earth for many months throughout the Northern Hemisphere. Incredibly, no human life was known lost, although all resident wildlife was obliterated.

Four years after the blast in 1916, a National Geographic Society Expedition led by Dr. Robert Griggs visited the region. What they found resembled an uninhabited planet light-years away or, as one party member wrote, "a devastated Lost Continent." Hot gases, mostly steam from superheated buried streams and springs, rose to the surface through countless cracks and tiny holes. Griggs named this valley, buried beneath a deep layer of ash with its myriad fumaroles, the "Valley of Ten Thousand Smokes."

A follow-up National Geographic Expedition in 1919 discovered that some of the fumaroles had disappeared and that the temperature was lower in others than it had been. By 1950 fewer than 100 "smokes" remained and today the active volcanic vents are all but gone. But to me the "Ten Thousand Smokes" name still seems appropriate for what once was, if not for what we now see. Few parks of the world offer a wilderness experience as profoundly moving or as fascinating.

One remarkable aspect is the way much of Katmai has recovered from the volcanic destruction of less than a century ago. Much of the park is green in summer, and the wildlife has returned. Within its boundaries is the meeting place of two life zones: Hudsonian, with forests of white spruce and dense stands of tall reedgrass, and Arctic, where only short grasses and low tundra plants grow. One morning when Peggy and I began a hike from our tent campsite on Naknek Lake to the summit of Dumpling Mountain, 2,440 feet above, we walked from one zone into the other.

The trek was exciting from the start. Barely five minutes beyond our tent, on a beach strewn with driftwood and hemmed in by spruce forest, we rounded a bend and came face to face with a very dark brown bear. It had been wading because it was dripping wet. With the usual soft, furry outline now smoothed and hard, the bear took on a much too sinister appearance for comfort. The bruin sat down in the water and looked away for a few seconds. We were starting slowly to turn back to find a detour when the bear stood up, shook itself, and then waded out to slightly deeper water. So it made its own deliberate detour around us. The beast never once seemed to really look at us, which is not uncommon with browns. But that doesn't mean it wasn't aware of us. From this point we moved more cautiously along the trail, which climbed away from the lakeshore, but we did not cross the paths of any more bears.

Above the woodland we came to an area of willows mixed with tall blue-joint grass (actually blue in color

If you fish along the Brooks River during spawning time, it's wise to watch for brown bears.

79

where leaves join the stem). At least 19 kinds of willow grow on the Alaska Peninsula. Moving along the trail we found ourselves in an area where moose had been browsing heavily, judging from the cropped appearance of the woody twig ends. That's when we discovered the bleached antler of a moose, discarded at least the previous autumn. Before I could pick it up to examine it, Peggy nudged me and pointed ahead. A bull moose, perhaps the same one that had dropped the old antler months ago, was munching, consuming the 50 pounds or so of green browse it would need daily to grow another set of antlers by early fall. (The bone antlers of this and other adult Alaskan bulls exceed the weight of an average person's skeleton. But whereas people need 18 years to grow a full-size skeleton, the moose needs only three or four months to produce his set of antlers. And he grows them annually!) Like the brown bear, this moose was so busy browsing that it barely looked at us in passing.

At first glance the tundra on Dumpling Mountain is similar to tundra in the Wyoming Rockies where we live. But the first tundra we encountered here was only about 1,000 feet above our camp and sea level. In Wyoming or Colorado we would have to climb to 9,000 feet or more to find the same plant community. In arctic Alaska, only 800 miles farther north than Katmai, we could find this same type of vegetation right at sea level.

Our climb up Dumpling Mountain had been accompanied by a cold drizzle and a raw wind. But when we neared the crest, there were breaks in the overcast and blue sky in the west. Then all at once we could see the entire length of the Brooks River far below, draining out of beautiful Brooks Lake and rushing about 2 miles and over 10-foot Brooks Falls, to empty into Naknek Lake. I especially enjoyed that view because I knew Brooks was among the finest fly-fishing rivers in a state full of them. We would be wading and casting in that water during the next day or two. To the northeast of Naknek Lake, the Bay of Islands was also becoming clearly visible. On a previous trip to Katmai, I had a day of unforgettable fishing there.

FISHING AT BROOKS. In the 1960s, I flew from King Solomon to Brooks Camp on a fishing trip. Brooks Camp, then as now, was isolated and not easy to reach. (Scheduled commercial airlines fly from Anchorage to King Salmon, summer population about 900, and from there it is a 35-mile hop by floatplane to a pumice beach beside Brooks Camp. If the weather is clear, the sightseeing on the flight from Anchorage over Lake Iliamna and several old volcanoes is stupendous.) My pilot was John Walatka. John was the

pioneer in bringing sport fishermen to this magnificent region by bushplane. He was also the manager of three lodges in the Katmai area for the owners, first Northern Consolidated, later Wien Airlines. To take full advantage of the long daylight during Alaska's summer, Walatka suggested that we make another brief flight into a certain secret lake he knew.

"It's called Idavain," he confided, "a landlocked lake not identified on many maps, a lake that almost nobody knows about. It has only one species of fish, easy to catch, so see if you know what they are."

Ten minutes later, John eased his plane to a soft landing on a lake surrounded by barrens and which I judged to be 3 miles long and a mile wide. He taxied toward a shallow beach, and in hipboots I jumped off the pontoon to tie an anchor line to willows on shore. We rigged fly rods, and waded out to knee depth to begin casting. Though my own first delivery was sloppy with too much haste and anticipation, a fish rose to the fly and hooked itself. I was too surprised to set the hook. John also had a strike. We soon landed identical gold-colored "trout," each about 14 inches long.

"I call them goldfins," John said, "for want of something better."

From the white edges on the pelvic and anal fins, it was evident the fish were chars rather than true trout. The backs were olive. But most unusual were the bright gold-scarlet bellies and flanks. I figured that these must be a race of Dolly Vardens that had become landlocked in this isolated lake long ago, when access to other waters was cut off. Perhaps it happened during the earthquakes and volcanic eruptions that shook Katmai in 1912.

Catching John's goldfins was almost as easy as laying some kind of fly into the water, so we filed the barbs off our hooks and kept none of the fish. Our largest was 18 inches long, but very thin, probably from stunting through overpopulation. John said he had once taken a 3-pounder, the largest he had seen there.

"But only a handful of people have ever wet a line here," John Walatka assured me.

That visit to Idavain took place two decades before I sat down to write this, so to me the present status of the remote lake is a mystery. John Walatka, the man who showed me so many other corners of wild Alaska, suffered a heart attack just as he was landing on another lake to sample the fishing there. He died in the cockpit, drifting with the wind toward a deserted shoreline, which might have been the way he wanted it.

For several days the weather around Brooks Camp was foul and I marked time. But when it improved ever so slightly, I joined a party of Michigan anglers on a fishing trip to the Bay of Islands, visible from atop Dumpling Mountain. It was a 1½-hour trip over rough water and into the teeth of a cold wind.

I shared a boat with Ed Jameson of Detroit and Bill Heise of Dearborn, Michigan. Our guide was Dick Pender, a native of Arizona who had recently found a new home in the Alaskan bush. Our destination was an archipelago, often windswept and gloomy, where the few rocky islands were evidence of many sunken reefs and hidden shoals. Pender had located some very big trout here, and we were about to have a sample of them. Most of the time the proper technique was to drift and cast over the reefs, but now the wind was so wild that this seemed impossible. Instead we decided to troll, and Dick set a course parallel to a steep, somewhat sheltered shoreline as we dropped our spinning lures overboard.

Bill Heise had the first action. He had hardly settled in his seat when he felt a sharp strike. Hooked solidly, the fish bored straight for the bottom of Naknek and stayed there. Applying all the pressure his tackle could stand, Bill regained his line only inches at a time.

"It's either a lake trout or an arctic char," Dick Pender said.

A few minutes later we had the answer. Pumping steadily, Bill maneuvered a fine laker close enough to the boat to be netted. It was certainly among the most colorful lake trout I had ever seen. They are normally silver-gray or sometimes brownish on the back. Like the Idavain Dolly Vardens, its flanks and fins were tinted golden, and I wondered about that similarity.

Like a gambler holding a hot hand, Bill Heise hooked and landed a second lake trout almost immediately, but lost a third one when his frayed line suddenly snapped. Then on his fourth strike, he hooked a heavy, acrobatic rainbow trout that leaped far out of Naknek Lake upon tasting the hook. Line literally screamed from Bill's reel, then abruptly went slack when the fish broke free.

My turn came next while Bill was examining his tackle for weak spots. The instant after I felt the strike another rainbow came out of the water, throwing spray. After that it made a wild run just beneath the lake's chop, almost as if not hooked at all. I worried about the ultralight tackle I was using. At the end of its run, the trout leaped again and then darted directly toward the bottom of the bay. Despite the cold and wild wind, I believe I was sweating beneath my parka.

The next few minutes brought on the kind of buck fever that infects even the most experienced fisherman. From watching the jumps, I knew my rainbow

John Walatka pioneered Alaska sport fishing by floatplane. He shows one of the small chars we caught in remote Idavain Lake.

was a trophy weighing about 10 pounds, which meant the struggle was far from over. You can't horse a fish such as that on monofilament line testing 6 pounds, so I payed out line on every run and gained some of it back whenever I could.

For the third time the trout surged to the surface, and this time we had a much closer look at it. No doubt about it, my rainbow was 10 pounds or better. But somebody noticed that it was only barely hooked in the corner of the jaw. One more jump would probably shake the hook free. Gently I applied pressure and Dick waited with the long-handled net.

Just 10 feet from the boat the fish wallowed and made a short run. At the end I was able to turn the fish and regain some line. Now with shaky hands I led the fish toward Dick who reached far out and made a pass with the net. That was like tossing a hand grenade in the water because the rainbow exploded and drenched me with cold spray. For a moment I couldn't tell if Dick had connected with the net or not. But the next thing I knew the rainbow was safely in the meshes, and Dick swung it aboard.

Later, back at Brooks Camp, the fish was weighed at 11½ pounds on honest scales. It was by far the largest rainbow I've even taken anywhere, twice as heavy as the next largest. Then and there I decided that I would probably never keep, or kill, another rainbow trout, no matter where or when I hooked it.

One 11½ pounder in a lifetime is anybody's just quota.

All of us had still more action there at Bay of Islands. Ed Jameson caught a rainbow and lake trout that were almost identical in size, at 9 pounds. I hooked another splendid rainbow and wasn't at all disappointed when it spit out the hook soon after. Late in the afternoon nobody actually wanted to reel in trolling lines and head back for Brooks, but the wind was increasing to storm velocity and a fine, cold rain stung our faces. Besides that we faced a long, bitter ride mostly across open water and again directly into the wind.

We needed two hours of pounding the waves and clutching the gunwales before scraping the beach again near camp. We were thoroughly stiff and chilled because some rain had managed to penetrate our foul-weather suits. Dick Pender's fingers were frozen stiff. But hot coffee, a hastily served warm meal, and warm sleeping bags corrected all that. Soon we forgot everything except the unbelievably good fishing at Bay of Islands.

When I awakened the next morning, bright sunlight was illuminating my tent. Reveling in the warmth, I turned over and probably was dozing off again when I heard activity and the other campers shouting. Unzipping my bag and looking out, I saw the reason for the commotion. A brown bear was walking through one corner of the campground. I was now wide awake. A bear in close proximity works better than any alarm clock.

KATMAI BEARS. Maybe even more than in the recent past, midsummer is the season of the bears, specifically of the giant Peninsula brown bears that are attracted to the annual spawning runs of sockeye salmon in the Brooks River and nearby streams of the Naknek drainage. There are a few better places in Alaska to see more bruins at even closer range than in Katmai Park, as on the McNeil River, which we'll explore later in this book, but Katmai is the most convenient, most accessible place to see the huge beasts in their wild and beautiful summer home.

In fact the abundance of bears in July has caused the National Park Service to enact more strict regulations for the Brooks Camp vicinity, and especially for the area surrounding Brooks Falls where most of the bears do their salmon fishing. Overlooking the falls a viewing platform has been erected to keep bears and people safely apart, but still within good viewing distance of one another. Rainbow trout and sockeye salmon fishing has been restricted to the stretch of Brooks River well below Brooks Falls.

The first time I fished the Brooks many years ago,

visitors and restrictions were few. I'd spend a few hours casting in the morning just below the falls, and the only other fishermen I would meet were bruins coming and going to that fertile fishing hole. I would often fly-cast near one bank of the river while a brownie or two splashed after sockeyes just opposite. Fishing was a much more interesting sport when you had to keep an eye on the competition which, roughly

speaking, weighed five times as much, could run a lot faster, and was immensely stronger. I also had to keep a wary eye to the rear because sometimes bears would approach the river from that direction. My strategy then was very simple: on spotting a bear I immediately relinquished my fishing rights.

It is often written that reds, or sockeye salmon, just in from salt water will not strike flies or artificial lures.

A brown bear cub, probably 2½ years old, waits patiently for its mother to begin fishing at Brooks Falls.

But the Brooks River is at least one spot where this is untrue. During the height of the run, when the reds were temporarily schooled below the falls, which they would try to jump upstream, they would strike

Left top: A brown bear splashes to shore with a salmon at Katmai. Left bottom: Red, or sockeye, salmon migrate in great numbers from the sea into many of the cold streams of Katmai to spawn. Their presence draws brown bears. Above, I show a good sockeye, and below son Bob hoists his sockeye catch.

brightly colored streamer flies of almost any pattern. Sometimes when we hooked a fresh 4- or 5-pounder in the fast water, we had to follow the fish downstream on foot, in order to net it far below. That also meant being careful not to run suddenly upon a bear sleeping off a big fish dinner in the dense brush on the bank. I did just that once and thereafter was cured of the practice. Shaken after stumbling within about 12 feet of one sleeper, I quit fishing for the day and found a spot on a bare bluff where I could just sit in peace and watch that lovely waterway flowing.

OTHER "FISHERMEN." What I found sitting on the bare bluff was that not all the fishermen on the Brooks River were bears or people. Another fisherman I noticed was a red fox that darted out from the brush along the far bank and began running crazily back and forth through a very shallow gravelly site. I could also see salmon flush away from the fox in all directions. Then suddenly the fox, scruffy looking from the summer moult, stopped running long enough to

notice a salmon that a sated bear had partially eaten and abandoned. The fox stalked it as if it were alive, then pounced on it and dragged the prize out of sight. I haven't seen another fox on the Brooks River, but I have seen them fishing unsuccessfully elsewhere.

Another morning I came to the falls area early and, when action was slow, sat down to watch and listen. The bears must have known that fishing was poor because none were in the immediate area. A yellow-legs waded, searching for larvae at water's edge, and a hermit thrush was baring its soul behind me, in contrast to the ravens, which only croaked. Then suddenly a wolf was on the scene.

Although more deliberate in its stalking method, the wolf was no better than the fox had been at catching sockeyes. Wading into deeper water, it would lunge at the dark shadows that flushed away from it. But at least this morning it caught nothing, and future prospects didn't seem good. (On another smaller stream in Katmai Park, ranger Rollie Ostermick did once see and photograph a wolf stalking and catching spawning salmon.) Very soon "my" wolf gave up and simply disappeared. Five minutes or so later I realized the reason. Two human anglers were slowly working their way upstream toward the falls, and the wolf's keener senses had alerted him long before I was aware of the approaching intruders.

From a high bank along the Brooks River, this red fox watched both me and a brown bear that was fishing. The instant the bear walked away, leaving a fish carcass behind, the fox retrieved it.

Later and far away, I wondered if this wolf at Brooks Falls was a member of the group I'd first met at Gros-venor-Coville narrows and later on the American River. The territory of a wide-ranging pack could conceivably have included all three places.

A further note on Katmai wolves is that although once frequently seen within the sanctuary's boundaries, today they make only very rare appearances. During the late 1970s Alaska Peninsula wolves were shot during winter by hunters in aircraft, some wolves being illegally taken within Katmai, where there is no law enforcement staff in the cold season.

THE ANIAKCHAK CALDERA NATIONAL MONUMENT. The same small, undermanned Katmai National Park staff also administers another extraordinary natural wonder on the Alaska Peninsula to the southwest, the 615,000-acre Aniakchak Caldera National Monument. Whereas several thousand people roam Katmai every summer, annual visitation at Aniakchak rarely exceeds a dozen curious outsiders. What they find is wildness as pure and exquisite as it can be.

The center of this monument is a 6-mile-in-diameter caldera, or collapsed crater, surrounded by the 4,000-foot walls of Aniakchak volcano, which last erupted in 1931. Inside the caldera is a snow-capped mountain and Surprise Lake, with turquoise-colored water, plus a moonscape of ash and cinder-fields colored yellow and black, maroon, and mahogany. Over this strange landscape brown bears and moose sometimes wander. The nearby totally wild coast supports sea lions and sea otters, harbor seals, and sea birds. In summer, salmon and sea-run trout abound in the Aniakchak River, which is floatable by raft or kayak. Anyone looking for his own great escape, for a wilderness of inhospitable beauty, virtually unknown and unlike any other on earth, might consider Aniakchak a perfect destination.

OTHER GREAT ESCAPES. This is the place to list some other great escapes in a state which has fewer residents than Columbus, Ohio. Most of the residents are concentrated in just a few sections of a landmass larger than France, Great Britain, Germany, and the Low Countries combined. A lot of places are labeled as frontiers or last frontiers by promoters and public relations types, but along with Antarctica, Alaska is the *true* last frontier on earth.

Covering the central portion of the Brooks Range on the "north slope" in subarctic Alaska is 8-million-acre Gates of the Arctic National Park, large enough that the region's wildlife communities are still complete and the food chain intact. As many as a quarter-million caribou may use and migrate through this park. Among its wild rivers are the challenging upper Kobuk, the 450-mile-long Noatak, which flows to the Arctic Ocean, and the more languid Alatna below Arrigetch Creek. I have not seen the Arrigetch Peaks, but do not doubt the friends who regard these as among the most spectacular of mountain massifs. Gates is four times as large as Yellowstone and the second largest national park ever established.

Wrangell–St. Elias of southcentral Alaska is the largest unit in the national park system and is greater still when considered as virtually one with adjoining Kluane National Park in Yukon Territory, Canada. Together they are included on the United Nations World Heritage List of most outstanding natural areas anywhere. But humans have left their indelible marks in this area of massive mountains and glaciers, in the form of mines and mining towns, mostly abandoned. Here, seven peaks exceed 14,500 feet, including Mt. St. Elias at 18,008 feet, the second highest peak on the continent. The highest is Mt. McKinley in Denali National Park. More than 100 glaciers here add up to the world's largest ice field beyond the polar regions. Dall sheep rams grow their heaviest horns in this park.

Four-million-acre Lake Clark National Park lies in the Chigmit Mountains, southcentral Alaska, where the Alaska Range meets the Aleutian Range. Fuming volcanos, Mt. Iliamna and Mt. Redoubt tower 10,000 feet over an alpine landscape drained by wild rivers. Access is by plane only, to Iliamna, then by charter 35 miles eastward into the park. Opportunities for exploring, hiking, river running, fishing, and wildlife watching are totally unlimited.

Kobuk Valley National Park is 40 miles north of the Arctic Circle and includes the dry, cold, 25-square-mile Great Kobuk Sand Dunes. Remote, seldom visited, breeding habitat for over 1,200 species of birds, this refuge contains remnant flora once common across the land bridge of tundra by which prehistoric men and many animal species crossed from Asia to Alaska.

The 300-square-mile Harding Ice Field, with its great glaciers, is the dominant feature of Kenai Fiords

Arctic ground squirrels, busy throughout the Katmai summer, play an important role in the ecosystem.

National Park, only a 125-mile drive from Anchorage, making it quite accessible. Hiking trails begin at Exit Glacier near Seward, but most access is by excursion or sight-seeing boat—to the Chiswell Islands, part of the Alaska Maritime National Wildlife Refuge as well. In fact one of the best, most convenient ways to see the wildlife of any Alaskan national park is by day-tripping into the fiords—Resurrection Bay, Aialik Cape, Aialik Bay, and other stunning places. Access is by one of the seaworthy vessels based in Seward. These boats are owned and run by Kenai Fiords Tours. On a typical day aboard, travelers will see sea otters, whales, sea lions, harbor seals, mountain goats, and thousands of seabirds within photographic range.

CHAPTER FIVE
Islands in the Arctic Mists

Late in 1784, just after the American Revolution, the sailing vessel *States* arrived at its home port of Boston with a most unusual cargo: 13,000 fur seal pelts from the faraway Falkland Islands. Few if any Bostonians of that era had ever even heard of the Falklands, which lie just east of southern Argentina, or of fur seals for that matter. But soon the golden-brown skins proved almost worth their weight in gold bullion, and a frantic worldwide race to obtain more of the exquisite pelts began.

Until this time fur seals and their seal rookeries were numerous in the Southern Hemisphere, some important ones being on Juan Hernandez Island, the South Shetlands, South Orkneys, Mas-a-fuero, Prince Edward Island, and the Antipodes, plus a few other lonely islands. But during the next five decades those rookeries were destroyed as quickly as they were discovered. New England and British skippers slaughtered the animals and hauled many millions of pelts to Chinese markets to be traded for silk, tea, and other products of the Orient. It is not surprising that the dawn of the 19th century found only a few fur seals still clinging to a precarious existence on earth. These were pitifully small herds on scattered coastal islands off South Africa, New Zealand, and in the Galapagos. But the demand for the hides was greater than ever.

It is fairly easy to see what effect these events and discoveries had on countries such as Imperial Russia, then trying to emerge as a world power. Desperately in need of foreign exchange, the empress Catherine the Great was intrigued by reports she had received from the North Pacific outposts. For some time her own Russian naval officers exploring the New World had noted great migrations each spring of huge numbers of fur seals through Unimak and other narrow

Depending on their bulk, age, and strength, fur seal bulls, after coming ashore on St. George in the spring, acquire harems of varing size from one or two cows to dozens.

passes of the Aleutian Islands. But beyond this bleak mysterious archipelago, the mammals just seemed to evaporate into the Bering Sea. A crash program to locate the seagoing mammals brought Russians in astonishing numbers into those arctic regions.

Among the Russian officers most determined to follow the seals to ancestral breeding grounds was one Captain–Commander Gerasim Pribilof, who had no interest whatever in wildlife per se or in natural history. Rather he realized that fame and fortune awaited anyone who found the bonanza. However that would not be easy in a part of the world where the foulest of weather was endemic. The weather's toll on Russian sailing ships and sailors for the past 40 years had been enormous.

No known written record survives to describe the day in 1786 that some deckhand aboard Pribilof's boat sighted land. No doubt the sudden presence of masses of seabirds screaming in the mist alerted the Russian that land was within reach. Possibly the towering cliffs and tundra-covered, extinct cinder cones were first glimpsed at dangerously close range and only intermittently through thick fog and scud, because it is almost always foggy and misty there.

Carefully, Pribilof approached near enough to one of two islands, now named after St. George and St. Paul, to hear seal bulls bellowing well before he could clearly discern their outlines on the rocky beaches. But no matter, the last and perhaps largest fur seal rookery of all on earth had been discovered at last.

What followed was pillage—slaughter—of the Pribilof herd in the manner followed by sealers at the opposite end of the globe. Here were untold riches for the taking. Aleuts were forced from their homes in the Aleutian Islands and transported north to these previously uninhabited islands just to kill and skin the seals for the Russians. That kill was limited only by how fast and efficiently the slaves could club and collect—females and pups included. By about 1834 the fur seals had been all but wiped out, as had the

sea otters and walruses of the Bering Sea earlier.

Fearful of losing the revenue, and not from conscience, the Russians belatedly banned killing females after that. But from the time of Pribilof's first beachhead until the sale of Alaska to the United States in 1867, a minimum of 3 million pelts were taken. At today's current values those skins would possibly be valued at from $5 billion to $6 billion. The eventual sale of Alaska to the United States may be the reason many fur seals (fewer than a million in 1987) still return each year to the two main islands, as well as Otter Island and a few nearby seal rocks.

But even after America purchased Alaska, the survival of northern fur seals hovered in grave doubt. Under U.S. jurisdiction, seal killing continued largely unregulated for many years. The first complete census made in 1912 revealed the existence of only 215,000 animals, and even this population was declining because hunting at sea continued, where many animals are killed and then lost. It was not until international agreements were signed, the last after World War II, that the future of the Northern Pacific fur seals was guaranteed. For their own mutual profit, Russia, Japan, Canada, and the United States agreed that the animals should be managed on a sound, scientific basis, that there should be no pelagic hunting (killing at sea), and that profits of the harvest should be shared equally by all signatories.

Fortunately this is one international agreement that has worked fairly well. Thereafter actual harvest was managed each summer on the Pribilofs by the U.S. Department of Commerce, which in recent years has succeeded the U.S. Department of the Interior, Bureau of Commercial Fisheries. In July of 1974, Peggy and I made our first journey to the Pribilofs to see the fur seals for ourselves.

THE NORTHERN FUR SEAL. What kind of creature is the northern fur seal, *Callorhinus ursinus?* A widely ranging mammal with 30 million years of evolution and experience in navigating open oceans, it is seldom seen alive except by commercial fishermen from Alaska southward to the Oregon coast, and by visitors to the Pribilofs and certain Asian islands near

A typical St. George rookery looks like this. Notice how the harems of the several larger, darker bulls are crowded together. No wonder that violent disputes often occur.

Siberia where the seals gather in summer. In addition to St. Paul, St. George, and Sea Lion Rock of the

Pribilof Islands, the animals also breed on Copper and Bering islands of the Commander group off Kamchatka, on Robben Island off Sakhalin, and on Kotikoviya and Srednevoya islands in the Kuriles. Fur seals had been exterminated from the latter two places by about 1890, but reappeared in small numbers in the 1950s. Still 80 percent or more of *all* northern fur seals are from the rookeries of the Pribilof Islands.

The young German naturalist Georg Wilhelm Steller, whom I mentioned earlier, was the first European to describe the fur seal. At dusk on August 10, 1741, while he was a member of an exploration voyage to mainland Alaska, Steller had observed the seals swimming near the ship and noted them in his journal. Then while shipwrecked the following summer on Bering Island, Steller watched astonished as the same mammals came ashore to breed. But it wasn't until after the naturalist's death at 37 that publication in 1751 of his "De Bestiis Marinis" introduced the northern fur seal to science and the western world. Among the facts Steller did not discover was that a fur seal pelt contains 30,000 hairs per square inch,

making it rich and luxurious beyond any other fur.

Nor did Steller note that fur seals have unusually large flippers compared with those of other seals and sea lions. This large flipper area permits cooling, especially on land, since the extremely dense fur effectively insulates other parts of the body. The fur is so impermeable to water that the skin underneath remains dry even as a seal rubs or scratches itself when swimming or diving. The animals do not completely molt. Normal body temperature is about 100°F, and overheating from unusual exertion or extended bright sunshine when on land causes considerable discomfort. Scientists have noted that if a fur seal's body temperature exceeds 107°F for any reason, the animal usually dies.

A fur seal's eyes are large and capable of gathering enough light to travel and feed at night. When at sea, in fact, the seals forage primarily after dark because some of their important food species rise to upper water layers after sundown. But being opportunists, they feed on whatever they can catch during the daylight hours, too: capelin and sand lance in the Bering

Left: On St. George we had to maneuver through the territory of bellowing bachelor bulls to reach a spot where we could photograph the west rookery. Above: A mother fur seal picks up a newborn that had wandered too far.

Sea, herring, pollock, rockfish, hake, squid, lanternfish, and, on occasion, salmon.

The seal has 36 teeth. Any fish grasped in these teeth has no chance to escape. The lower incisors fit into a notch in the upper incisors, and the upper molar and premolar teeth interlock with the lower, making a most efficient bite. In a dive, the nostrils of a fur seal close. The external ears are small, tightly rolled cylinders with a narrow, waxy orifice that keeps water from entering.

Pups, which weigh from 10 to 12 pounds at birth, grow into either mature females weighing 95 to 110 pounds, or into mature bulls that weigh from 400 to 600 pounds. Average adult females measure about 56 inches from nose to tip of tail; bulls average 7 feet long. This startling size difference between the sexes is apparent even before birth. In one study in May unborn male fetuses measured about an inch longer and a half pound heavier than females. When dropped on a St. Paul beach, a typical male pup is about 26 inches long, an inch or two longer than a female.

The midsummer wildflower show on the Pribilofs is always exquisite. The lupine is one of the most common wildflowers.

At sea females and young males are metallic gray in color. Once ashore on the Pribilofs, however, they appear yellow-brown, almost golden, in the rare bright arctic sunshine, but often become discolored by the dark earth and excrement in the rookeries. Pups are shiny black at birth, but become gray by September. Bulls over six years old are predominantly brownish black, with some dark gray and reddish brown individuals. Fully grown males develop short, bushy manes on muscular shoulders and neck. Today anyone with an interest in these splendid marine mammals can see them by visiting the Pribilof Islands.

THE PRIBILOFS. In 1974 two scheduled flights a week from Anchorage via Cold Bay at the western tip of the Alaska Peninsula were made by Reeve Aleutian Airways, a small carrier founded and operated by pioneer Alaska bush pilot Bob Reeve. Now dead, Reeve remains an aeronautic legend in Alaska. We scheduled our trip for midsummer and what we discovered 188 years after the Russian explorer Pribilof went ashore in a long boat is well worth describing. Considering international events in between, including two World Wars and the Korean conflict, we were surprised that any wilderness at all survived in such a strategically important place halfway between the world's two most powerful and often distrustful nations.

Our flight by vintage DC-6 aircraft, veteran of who knows how many arctic flights, was less than luxurious. But once aboard we enjoyed more leg room and comfort per passenger than is available on commercial aircraft. Most of our fellow passengers were members of a Massachusetts Audubon Society nature tour, and we occupied only part of the cabin. The remainder was filled with cargo, securely lashed in place wherever it fit best. The flight, delayed 2 hours because our destination was completely socked in by fog, required 2½ hours and passed within awesome view of Mt. Redoubt and Mt. Iliamna, both peaks over 10,000 feet. It also flew over Lake Iliamna and Pavlof Volcano. On a rare clear day we would have enjoyed breathtaking views from the windows, but this time could see only a gray featureless void.

Emerging suddenly from a soggy overcast, we landed on St. Paul about noon, and for those arrivals who had never seen an arctic landscape before, the scene around the "airport" was a severe shock. The tallest living plants were clumps of purple lupine which, bowing to a stiff wind and stinging rain, were nowhere more than a foot high. There we saw our first Pribilof birds: snow buntings.

All visitors to St. Paul then stayed at "the hotel," a spartan, weathered, frame accommodation operated by the Aleut community, descendants of those enslaved by the Russians generations earlier. Whenever the hotel was full, a nearby barracks built originally for the military was used. During our four-day sojourn Peggy and I found a barracks squad room to be entirely comfortable and had the nearly empty facilities to ourselves.

Now remember that beyond the edge of this one community of people, and a Coast Guard Loran Station not far away, St. Paul is uninhabited. To explore this barren real estate we had to scrounge for transportation which was almost nonexistent, in order to travel on the few rough gravel roads which mostly lead to Tolstoi, Kitovi, and other lonely seal beaches. A few of the residents owned Honda motorbikes. A battered yellow school bus was reserved to transport the Audubon group. Luckily, and thanks to the Aleut community leaders, Peggy and I were able to rent an ancient van in which to wander. Its battery was about exhausted and the transmission uncooperative, but for our exploration needs, that rusting Ford proved as valuable as our binoculars and cameras.

For anyone not thrilled by scenes of stark and barren wilderness beauty, of gray-green seascapes filtered through drizzle and dampness, often without definite horizons, St. Paul is a poor place to be "trapped" for a week or so. True enough there was the old seal-pelt curing and processing plant to visit, but that is a dank and depressing place at best. Sts. Peter and Paul Russian Orthodox Church, founded in 1880 (the present structure being rebuilt in 1903), might be more interesting for some, but unaccountably it was kept locked. So was the marine fisheries laboratory in town throughout our stay. But we would have felt it a gross waste of time to waste any valuable daylight indoors. Besides, for one entire day and part of a second, we enjoyed the most precious commodity in the Pribilof part of the Bering Sea: sunlight.

FUR SEALS OF ST. PAUL. From town we drove first to a seal beach about a mile away. A sheltered stone blind overlooking a rocky shore made this both the handiest and most popular seal-watching site on the island.

Here the sight of massed, mating fur seals was extraordinary. Nowhere else in North America, except possibly at Carlsbad Caverns, New Mexico, during the evening exodus of clouds of bats, is it possible to stand in one place and see so many mammals at one time, or to find so many focused in the viewfinder at once. This and nearby seal rookery beaches seethed

Action and conflict never cease in a fur seal rookery as bachelor bulls come ashore to try to take territories and harems from established bulls. Overleaf: We shot this scene of a major northern furseal rookery on St. Paul Island in 1974. Since then the number of the seals has fallen alarmingly.

with life, with thousands of golden fur coats of the adults interspersed with smaller ebony ovals that were the newborn pups. But in early July the fur seals were not just lolling in the comparative warmth of the brief Alaskan summer. We soon discovered that there is constant activity, some of it violent. And the activity is accompanied by an unending din of bellowing, barking, and the small squeals of the infant seals. Add to this an all-pervasive animal odor that might be flatteringly described as fishy (although this was only one facet of the smell), and you can better appreciate the scene.

By the first of July, well before we had arrived, the beachmasters, or harem bulls, have already been ashore for a least a month, and the dominant bulls, that may have arrived first, have already established themselves in the best possible beach sites, those at water's edge where the females will later come ashore.

Some of the most awesome males manage harems of 25 or 30 and occasionally even more. They defend their territories and keep the harem segregated in a knot away from other bulls that occupy less strategic territories. They also drive off bulls that just roam the periphery hoping to find a willing, undefended female. Here and there sits a bull with only one or two cows, and perhaps another bull waiting his chance to move in and breed.

But as long as any females in the vicinity remain to come into estrus, there is constant, noisy conflict, with battle-scarred bulls trying to move in on one another's property. And of course savage fights occur, and blood flows from new wounds on the swollen necks of the antagonists. We saw this happen time and again.

Very soon after the females come ashore, small and silky black pups of 10 or 12 pounds each are born. And shortly after the birth, the cows come into season and mate again. This is a curious sight, too, because the males weigh five times as much as their mates. Between the birthing, fighting, and mating, we found uninterrupted turmoil almost wherever we wandered

over St. Paul's beaches. Most of the time it seemed unreal, occurring as it did on those misty, cold shores drenched by ocean spray. The sights, sounds, and smells were often blended together by the vagaries of the weather.

We could easily see that the mortality of the pups in those overcrowded rookeries is very high. We saw the life suddenly squeezed out of one squalling pup as copulating adults, unknowning and uncaring, rolled on top of it. Peggy and I also watched a bull that had just come out second best in an encounter with a beachmaster bull take out its frustration on a nearby pup. Repeatedly he grabbed the pitiful young one by the throat, shook it as a bulldog shakes a rat, and tossed it high into the air, allowing it to crash to the ground. The bull continued this long after the tiny victim was dead. A short time later one of the numerous foxes of St. Paul showed up to feed on the carcass, which was too heavy to drag to a nearby den. What carcasses foxes do not consume are quickly eaten by the ever-present gulls.

Most of the few tourists to St. Paul each summer are restricted to visiting only one or two of the rook-

Previous page: Though battles are common, some bulls may be unable to secure rights to even a single cow. Above: This bull attempts to steal a cow bodily from another harem. The result was a fight with the former owner.

eries for several reasons. (One is near the weatherproof stone blind mentioned earlier.) Some beaches located on remote parts of the island are not easily accessible by the old school bus. Also there is a safety measure. In the past, some foolish camera-toting travelers have approached breeding bulls too closely and courted serious trouble. Most males will defend their territories with terrible zeal, no matter who or what intrudes. But mostly this restriction of tourists to certain areas was designed to allow the summer harvest of seals to proceed unobserved and unimpeded. For the majority of outsiders, the harvest wouldn't be a pleasant thing to watch.

On a typical day during the old July sealing harvest, a crew of 20 to 50 experienced Aleut sealers proceeded to a beach and there surrounded a large herd, while trying to cut off escape to the sea. Three- and four-year-old bulls were separated from all others as much as possible, then driven to an open "killing field" on the tundra. There all animals of desired size and good pelage were quickly dispatched by clubbers with a single blow to the head.

Of course this killing method was the subject of great controversy, and many other methods were tested. But clubbing remained the quickest and most efficient means, in addition to being the most humane when done by the experienced Aleuts. Each year about 50,000 young males were harvested in that way. These were considered as the annual surplus that was safe to remove. At that time, during the early 1970s, the northern fur seal population was maintaining its numbers at a constant high level, which might have been the maximum the Bering Sea environment could support. Today biologists don't know for sure what the maximum really is.

ST. PAUL'S SEABIRD ROOKERIES. But we found another wildlife treasure on St. Paul that almost matched our intimate glimpses of a fascinating marine mammal. We also thrilled to one of the finest mixed seabird rookeries on this continent or anywhere else.

Many such seabird colonies from the Bering Sea to Baffin Island contain one or two or even three species nesting at any one time. Here, while hiking alone along the thin edge of a mile-long cliff overlooking the rolling gray sea, Peggy and I counted a dozen. For the record, our list included common and thick-billed murres; black- and red-legged kittiwakes; horned and tufted puffins; least, parakeet, and crested auklets;

Left: Two beachmasters are disputing territory. As seen in the bottom photo, in the heavy traffic battling bulls may inadvertently crush and kill pups.

Tufted puffins nest in cliff crevices, or in burrows, or on rocks with the murres. They are part of one of the world's finest seabird rookeries.

pelagic and red-faced cormorants; and fulmars. We found all of these on one particular cliff face along the western shore of St. Paul.

Even more noteworthy than the galaxy of seabirds was the convenience of reaching their rookery. In a career devoted largely to wandering around the world to hunt wildlife with a camera, I can recall few similar places so easily accessible. Just by riding the school bus and then walking to a finger of land, anyone can look to an adjacent headland and watch the comings and goings of hundreds of marine birds. All of them are busy with nest building and chick-rearing on narrow ledges on the edge of eternity.

In one place Peggy found a pair of puffins sitting on a rock about 300 feet directly above an angry, gray surf—colorful birds in a splendid ocean setting. Of all seabirds present here, the puffin is the strangest looking, with its huge parrot beak. To get as close as possible for pictures, I crawled infantry-style on my belly to the very edge. Peggy held on to my ankles to prevent any accident. Then looking straight down, I stared directly into the face of an equally astonished blue arctic fox. How any four-footed animal without

wings ever reached that thin ledge is more than I can explain. Apparently it had mastered cliff climbing to better harvest the bounty of seabird eggs and chicks. Later, around the entrance to several summertime fox dens, we could determine the fox family diet by the feathers and remains of different nesting birds.

Despite the accessibility of the island, hikers atop bird cliffs can still easily imagine they are on the loneliest island on earth. The wilderness scene has changed little since Pribilof arrived and for centuries before that. A northwest wind whines against cracks and crevices. Low clouds come drifting in at water level below, totally obscuring any view of the ocean. The clouds are wet on your face, and the lupine blooms and their hairy stems are covered with water droplets. This isolates a person on a small tundra island where even the cries of the seabirds nearby are muted and sound distant. Being there on St. Paul, we had an ideal chance to experience what existence might be like on an arctic ocean, second only to being on the deck of a rolling ship.

THE PRIBILOFS TODAY. Nowadays the human population of the Pribilofs fluctuates between 400 and 500. With a drastic decline in both fur seals and birds, and summer sealing discontinued, many islanders are busy accommodating a slowly increasing number of visitors. They are building boat docks and airstrips. And there is exploration for minerals. But weather makes all these occupations very seasonal.

In 1974 much activity centered around the post office, with a postmistress, and a village commissary, where rock music blared incessantly. The merchandise was varied, fresh, and in good supply, although very expensive.

A sign in the post office read: "It is unlawful to molest postal employees when on duty." A bulletin board in the commissary requests all to always "buy enough beer *before* weekends. Anyone calling clerks for beer after closing time will be summoned before the town council." We wondered who protected the postal workers when they were *not* on duty, and how busy the council must have been after a normal weekend, say in January, or after New Year's Eve. Plenty busy it would appear, judging from the number of discarded beer and pop cans that littered the town.

Flying back to Anchorage, following that long-ago

Top: Almost all of the red-legged kittiwakes in the world nest in rookeries on the cliffs of one island, St. George. Bottom: The Pribilof Islands are a major nesting area for thick-billed murres. The nesting areas are always noisy and busy.

trip, with any last look at the Pribilofs made impossible by a soupy overcast, we had a final chance to reflect on what we had seen on one of America's most remote outposts.

So far I've hardly mentioned the wildflower "show" that was incredibly beautiful and memorable to even the least sensitive visitor. Vast areas of lupine and lousewort, of moss campion, heather, primrose, and avens, some unique to the Pribilofs, brightened the low-key beauty of St. Paul during the endless days of midsummer. In scattered places when sunlight could pierce the overcast, the tundra seemed aglow. We considered this, the bird life, and of course, the fur seals. But probably it was the seal harvest, the annual seal killing that most occupied our thoughts.

THE SEAL HARVEST. It was true that the northern fur seal was then doing well, and we'd have been gratified indeed if all the world's species were faring half as well. But in my trip notes I wondered how to justify the mass killing, which only furnished fur coats for a few of the world's wealthiest people. Was providing a livelihood for native people a sufficient rationale? In these days of expanding international tourism and growing concern about world wildlife, would this remarkable ocean resource be worth more as a destination for naturalists and photographers than as a giant fur farm? Do the fashionable people of the world really need genuine fur coats? Would the Pribilofs be a vastly more valuable natural asset as a wilderness national park, maybe even as an *international* park, since the fur seals of summer also spend part of their lives in the waters of Canada, Japan, and the Soviet Union?

Answers to some of the above questions have been provided, but these have raised still others. Except for very limited sealing for native subsistence, the harvest has been discontinued, partly because seal coats are now out of fashion, but mainly due to great alarm over the suddenly diminishing size of the fur seal herd. The total number of animals returning to the Pribilofs in 1987 was not much higher than when scientific management was begun. What happened? We know that one of the reasons is that a terrible toll is taken by the nets of the international fishing fleet that infests those arctic waters. The spreading cancer of pollution of the seas may be another reason. More about these problems later.

ST. GEORGE. In July 1987 Peggy and I had the chance to return to the Pribilofs for a firsthand look, this time not to St. Paul, but to seldom-visited St. George, the larger of the two main islands.

Walk along any beach beneath the ocean cliffs and you will find pairs of horned puffins perched on ledges decorated with colorful arctic lichen.

One thing besides the decline of wildlife that had greatly changed during the 13-year interval was the transportation to the islands. In 1974 traveling to St. George, population about 125, would have meant flying first to St. Paul (as we did), and then waiting to catch a small shuttle aircraft that could occasionally make the short 45-mile hop southeastward when neither island was closed in by weather. In 1987 our party of eight boarded a twin-engine Cessna Conquest in Anchorage at 0930. Flying at 300 mph and in the usually clear skies above 28,000 feet, with a single fuel stop in King Salmon on the Alaska Peninsula, we touched down on St. George three hours later, 780 miles west of Anchorage. The day was gray and drizzly, and the bleak airstrip was still unimproved. Some things never change. We checked into the quaint white-painted St. George Hotel, recently designated a National Historic Landmark. After a light lunch we were photographing puffins on a sea cliff only about a 5-minute walk distant.

Any outdoorsperson can visit the island on his own, by making plans and reservations with the St. George Tanaq Corporation, based in Anchorage. There is usually space available on some of the frequent flights. And you can rent the single van with a guide to take you around the approximately 15-square-mile island. But we're convinced that by far the best way to visit the Pribilofs is to join an organized nature tour or all-expense package photography tour, as led by Joseph Van Os of Vashon Island, Washington. An experienced naturalist, Van Os is especially familiar with travel in wilderness Alaska.

As a local guide on St. George, Van Os had engaged Greg McGlashan, a wiry and enthusiastic man with a wide employment background as a wildlife (fur seal) technician, commercial fisherman, sealer, deputy wildlife officer, and heavy equipment operator. All this in a life of only 40 years. McGlashan's great-grandfather, a seaman on a Scottish whaling boat, had jumped ship in 1870 at Akutan in the Aleutian Islands, married a native woman, and begun a new life. Born on St. George, Greg, with a zest for learning anything at all and a high energy level, knows the place and the inhabitants intimately, human and wild. Despite the intermittent drizzle and seldom-broken overcast, he saw to it that we made the most of four days in a rich wildlife sanctuary.

St. George does not have nearly as many fur seals as St. Paul, and some beaches that would have been alive with breeding animals only a few years ago were now bare. The population of seabirds is also down, although not so drastically. Still, for its size, St. George is probably the largest summer seabird colony

We spent time around this den of arctic foxes, and eventually the wary kits became accustomed to us. One of the parents delivered this murre to the den, left immediately, and barked at us from a distance.

in the Northern Hemisphere, and it surely rates among the world's premier bird sights.

On precipitous cliffs that loom as high as 1,000 feet, is the largest colony of thick-billed murres in the North Pacific. They're a shifting, fluttering, swooping mass of millions. St. George is believed to be the world's largest breeding site of parakeet auklets and a major breeding area for crested and least auklets. Nearly the entire world population of red-legged kittiwakes nest here on sheer cliff walls. Seeing and photographing all these birds is sometimes dizzying and always an exhilarating experience.

Surprisingly, one of our most interesting encounters was neither with the birds nor the fur seals. One morning during a brief, cold rain we huddled beneath a cliff overhanging a black-sand beach. We checked frequently to see that the cameras were protected from the moisture. That's when we noticed a scruffy, blue-phase arctic fox walking along the beach studying the rookeries above as it traveled. Suddenly it darted toward a cliff face not far away and began climbing, eventually out of our sight. We could follow its progress only by the flushing and squawking of the birds in its path. In a few moments the fox was back down on the beach with a limp murre in its mouth. It then turned and trotted away around a bend at water's edge. When the rain stopped, we followed.

The fox's tracks in the dark sand were easy to follow for a few hundred yards. Then they turned abruptly inland toward a huge jam of driftwood washed high onto the island by storms at sea. At the edge of the jumble of timber I saw the white breast of the murre and several tiny fox kits scrambling to get out of sight and safely underground. We had located the den of

105

An arctic fox prowls at the base of bird-nesting cliffs, alert for any opportunity to grab a chick, eggs, or an unwary adult. These island foxes have become excellent climbers.

one of the numerous arctic foxes living on St. George. Sitting on a bleached log at telephoto lens distance from the opening, we set up tripods and waited until two of the smoke-colored kits emerged and tried to drag the murre carcass inside.

Several times during our stay, Peggy and I returned to that fox den to photograph the kits, and in time they seemed to lose some of their fear of us. There were six kits, not just the two we had seen at first. One of the parents, probably the mother, did not share her mate's tolerance of our presence. Whenever she

murres. At such close range these colonies assault the senses. Here were 700 to 800 murres nearby, with thousands more just beyond, in rows shoulder to shoulder on the narrow ledges, extending from near the beach below to the top of the cliff high above. There was no pause in the noise they made. Every arrival or departure to and from feeding expeditions precipitated a spate of honking from all the birds in the immediate vicinity. Encroachment inevitably occurred and was dealt with even more noisily. Like all such colonies, this one never slept. Throughout the 24-hour daylight of midsummer in the Bering Sea, the turmoil goes on uninterrupted. The silence in late summer when all the birds have gone must seem eerie indeed.

The murres and many other species of seabirds establish these immense colonies in areas that enable them to meet three basic needs: breeding, feeding, and security. The steepest, least accessible cliffs are favored as protection against foxes and, elsewhere, against other land predators. As we saw, an agile, enterprising fox still manages to get into some of the not quite vertical cliff sites; otherwise the fox itself will starve. We were also in a good position to see why murres need cliffs with ledges, very narrow as they may be. The blue eggs are pear-shaped, pointed on one end, so that they don't fall from the ledges except in cases of extreme disturbance. Instead they roll in a tight circle, the narrow end hardly moving.

Of course the murres must have a sufficient supply of food: sculpins, capelin, cod, sand eels, or amphipods—within commuting distance of any nesting cliffs. The nearer, the better. Thick-billed murres are able to fly up to two hour's distance each way to feed and find enough to supply their young. The survival rates of the chicks may be higher if the foraging trips are shorter. Murres are able to dive 300 feet underwater and remain there for one to two minutes.

From our vantage, we noticed that the murres tended to depart separately, at random, on feeding flights. But often they arrived and departed in groups. Probably when they found a promising food source in the sea, all would leave for their share. I wondered what would happen to these remarkable birds if a catastrophic oil spill occurred and eliminated a summer's food supply.

On the afternoon of July 4th, when the St. George villagers were getting ready for their traditional dance, bonfire, and holiday celebration, the sun threatened to break briefly through the low, leaden clouds. Greg McGlashan drove us toward the North Rookery for a final look at the fur seals. Parking the van near the island's airstrip, we cut across the rolling terrain on

returned to the den from foraging and found us nearby, she would sit in full view on a distant log and bark incessantly. As long as she barked, the kits remained out of sight, and we would soon leave to walk along the lofty bird cliffs.

One afternoon we came upon a deep cleft in a rock face where we could perch on one side and look directly across at the seemingly solid mass of thick-billed

Prized for their pelts, fur seal bulls lead a life of constant strife on the Pribilofs. Those
not selected for harvest by the Aleuts make life difficult for one another.

foot, stalking through coarse, tall grass and gardens of lousewort, lupine, avens, and primrose. The walking isn't easy because the tangle of wildflowers covers a carpet of cannonball-size rocks.

Coming over a rise not far from the sea, we were suddenly confronted by a young fur seal bull that had been forced by more dominant bulls to stake a territory away from the most desirable area. "Out of the high-rent district," according to our guide. The bull looked at us uncertainly, barked, and made a short lunge straight for us. We backed off, detoured around it and walked directly into the domain of another young male. This one also charged. By broken field dodging, with backpacks full of heavy photo equipment swinging, we eventually reached the crest of the low cliff overlooking North Rookery. Like all such haulouts in July, this one was in constant turmoil.

With hundreds of fur seals in view, most of them continually agitated, we found it difficult to concentrate or focus cameras very long on any single spot. At one point I was watching as a pup was born in the center of a circle of females. While the mother was licking and gently moving the new arrival, a violent fight between two large harem bulls broke out much nearer to where I stood. They thrust head to head, striking at exposed necks and shoulders with long, sharp incisors until blood ran on both. They also fought dangerously close to where a school of sleek, black young pups huddled together, trying to avoid being crushed beneath the huge bulls.

McGlashan said that a good many young are killed in just this way each season. Out of the corner of my eye I noticed the arctic fox patrolling the area, just in case that happened. A minute later I saw the fox trotting off with the placenta of a recently born pup. At any given spot in a fur seal rookery, birth, death, and mating can take place simultaneously.

There were even rare times when, for a moment or two, the rookery would fall strangely quiet. Once during such a lull, as I stopped for a deep breath and to check the film in my camera, I saw a giant beach-master bull lurch heavily toward a harem at the base of the cliff just below me. Almost faster than a camera could record, it snatched a much smaller female from the group and turned to leave with her in his jaws. But the cow's "owner," caught dozing, reacted quickly and bit down on her flipper to prevent the abduction. Then began a brutal tug-of-war that ended only when the female's skin actually split at the base of the flipper and the interloper gave up his hopes of conquest. Then another fight erupted on the far side of the rookery. I couldn't recall ever witnessing a noisier or more violent Fourth of July.

I wondered about mortality in the rookeries and especially about pup mortality. According to Mc-Glashan, over the years 10 to 30 percent of all pups are dead before the southward autumn migration. Mortality results from starvation, physical injuries (bulls killing or rolling over pups), congenital defects, and infections. Not much is known about causes of death while at sea. Killer whales and great white sharks are known predators of seals of all ages, but mostly of the smaller individuals. Parasites probably kill some and weaken others so that they become easier prey of the whales and sharks.

Emaciated young seals that drift ashore in winter suggest that inadequate food and the violent weather of the region are the greatest hazards during a pup's first year at sea. During this period pups must make the sudden transition from nursing to finding their own food in a hostile and stormy winter ocean. Sometimes 85 percent of the pups fail to reach three

years, the age at which they are harvested for their pelts.

Among the saddest things I saw during my last day on St. George Island were fur seals doomed to die for no good reason at all. One of these was a female that had managed to drag herself out onto a rocky shore where two beachmasters met in a savage duel for her. But they were wasting their energies because their prize was hopelessly enmeshed in a section of green nylon fishing net, the legacy of a foreign fishing vessel far out at sea.

Not far down the shore another entangled cow that had managed to reach land was being recycled by a band of glaucous-winged gulls. McGlashan assured me the derelict nets are a far more serious problem than I could possibly see standing on that remote island cliff. He and his companions sometimes succeed in cutting seals free of the nets, but often the strands have cut too deeply, and the seals are too weakened to survive.

The next afternoon, safely back in Anchorage, Peggy and I checked into the Puffin Inn, wallowed in a hot shower, and enjoyed a deep-fried fresh halibut dinner. But it was disturbing to be in the noise and bustle of that busy place. I wished we were back in one of the wilder parts of Alaska. Early the next morning, we loaded up our VW van and aimed it northward toward Denali National Park.

CHAPTER SIX

A Fantastic Walrus Island

It is either sunset or sunrise when I am awakened from a deep sleep. I am not certain which because in mid-July along the Bering Sea the sun disappears only briefly below the horizon, and one end of the day looks much like the other. Our tent is pitched on a high island cliff overlooking Bristol Bay. Quickly I recognize the grunting and blowing sounds that awakened me as those of walruses returning to the island from a feeding trip far out to sea.

But there is also another sound—an almost unreal sound. Sometimes faint and sometimes fairly loud, it resembles far-away chimes, or perhaps chords played on an out-of-tune piano. These sounds come to me dreamlike, but then I remember that this strange belling is another sound made by bull walruses. Scientists still do not know its significance, except that it may be done mostly when males are displaying for females. Belling is produced by air expelled past vocal chords.

Peggy is also awake now, and we crawl from our warm double sleeping bag. A scarlet sun is just emerging over the eastern horizon, bathing our whole world in a glow as unearthly as the sound of the chiming. Looking over the edge of the cliff, we see the bellers. Almost a hundred huge animals have made a beachhead on the narrow strip of land just below, which was completely unoccupied when we retired a few hours earlier.

Welcome to Round Island, Alaska.

Even among Alaska's countless, scattered, remote wildlife islands, Round is unique. Little more than 2 square miles in area, usually hidden in the arctic mists, it is the hauling-out place, the temporary summer headquarters, for almost all the male Pacific walruses that survive on earth. From early June until the end

This is a typical, small haulout beach for walruses not far from our Round Island campsite. We took this photo on one of the region's rare, sunny days.

SELECTED SITES FROM THIS CHAPTER

of August from 10,000 (recently) to about 15,000 bulls (in the 1970s) gather to pack the narrow gravel beaches as tightly as a can of sardines. They average 1½ tons each, some reach 2 tons, and 10 feet in length. Probably nowhere on earth, not even where elephant herds still walk, is so much biomass packed per acre of solid ground.

111

I saw Round Island for the first time when flying over in a seaplane in summer, 1965. The spectacle from above was overwhelming—so many giant mammals jammed onto a thin strip of beach between surf and sea cliffs. Because the day was uncommonly calm for that part of the world, and because the ocean surface seemed nearly flat, the pilot decided to "land" for a closer look. Touching down on swells we could not see from above, we bounced wildly and taxied onto a stretch of unoccupied beach. Then for an hour or two, before the sky suddenly darkened and the wind picked up ominously, I was able to hike close to the massed walruses and expose all the film I carried. The pilot, who flew a small bush plane, part of a now-defunct charter business, was immensely relieved once we were airborne again. He said that there were only two or three days every year when a pilot in his right mind would think of landing at Round Island as we had just done.

That was a memorable day. And I always hoped to go back somehow, not only for a better, longer look at the animals, but also to see the incredible seabird nesting colonies I'd glimpsed on the sheer cliffs.

But Round Island simply is not an easy place to visit. Except for a caretaker-biologist or two in summer, it is uninhabited. It is far from anywhere, the closest community being the cannery village of Togiak, 70 miles away round-trip by boat. With no suitable sheltered anchorages anywhere around the island, the normally angry ocean allows transfer from boat to shore by inflatable raft only part of the time. High winds, rain, and penetrating cold are endemic to Round Island, and anyone who ventures there had better be prepared to stay longer than planned. Summer visitors have been marooned on the island for as long as 10 days after having tents blown away in gales of near cyclone force. I knew these things, but still yearned to see that lonely outcropping of real estate again and photograph it.

The chance came in 1987. Joseph Van Os, a young naturalist who runs a busy travel service for wildlife addicts, was organizing a July expedition for about a dozen of the most serious. The timing proved of incredible good fortune, because for four days we enjoyed uninterrupted sunshine. Winds were moderate, and daytime temperatures above 70°F. This is what is expected in the South Seas, not Round Island. But even under the best of conditions, reaching Round can be tedious business.

It begins with a 2-hour scheduled jet flight from Anchorage to Dillingham, a weathered outpost town southwest of where the Wood and Nushagak rivers empty into Bristol Bay. From Dillingham our group of 12 shuttled in two segments by Otter aircraft to land on a thin strip of cleared gravel beach beside a salmon cannery at Togiak. We had dinner with the cannery employees in their dining room and spent the short night in the spartan cannery bunkhouse.

Don Winkleman, a Togiak fur trapper in winter and salmon fisherman in summer, today provides the only reliable link to Round Island with his 24-foot outboard runabout, *Puffin II*. Winkleman planned to transport our party and our considerable amount of gear in two round-trips, each requiring about 4 hours. The trips were timed to take best advantage of the high-tide period. Peggy and I waited for the second of the shuttles and this gave us a chance to watch and photograph the great number of seabirds—black-legged kittiwakes, glaucous-winged gulls, arctic and Aleutian terns, long-tailed and parasitic jaegers—that fed madly on offal discharged from the cannery.

Reaching Round Island was no trouble over a choppy sea alive with murres and puffins, kittiwakes and guillemots. Nor was getting ashore, two at a time, in a small, inflatable raft. But manhandling our gear from water's edge to the top of a 100-foot cliff, by fireman's ladder, and then backpacking it to the single, nearly level site suitable for camping (with a trickle of drinking water available) was another matter. Once six tents were pitched and all gear in place, Peggy looked at her wristwatch and at the sky. "Let's not waste time here," she said, "let's go to the walruses while the sun is shining. It may not last long."

WALRUSES. From camp we could look westward toward the tip of the island where most of the walruses were hauled out and near where I had landed long ago. But a smaller haulout beach was located less than half that distance east of our cliff-top camp, and we decided to hike to this one instead. In the daylight still remaining we loaded cameras, lenses, and tripods into backpacks and then headed out to one of the thin, steep trails that radiate outward from camp to other points on the island.

In camp the terrain seemed gentle. But this was deceptive, and we needed more than 30 minutes to negotiate the half mile or so through coarse, thigh-high, Calamagrostis grass and wildflowers. Then we reached the edge of a high cliff from which the trail curved downward to the edge of a remarkable scene. Directly below us 800-odd walruses were jammed flipper to flipper on a shore much smaller than a football

Top right: Walrus bulls hold crowded, jostling conventions. Bottom: Bulls are distinguished from females by their larger bulk, broader muzzles, heavier tusks, and numerous large tubercles on necks and shoulders.

field. Many more cavorted in the water nearby. It was one of those times when I have trouble setting up equipment because of the five thumbs on each hand.

We watched and photographed the spectacle that evening until the beach and all its inhabitants were darkened by the growing shadow of the cliff on which we stood. Even then we sat quietly for a while and listened to the grunting, to the constant disputes of so many pinnipeds packed so close together. The hike back to camp seemed almost easy. During the night we awoke and heard the walruses reclaiming the exact spot where we had landed on the island.

Walruses are the largest members of the widely distributed family of marine mammals, including all seals and sea lions, called pinnipeds (from pinna, a fin; and pedis, a foot). Their original geographical range included mostly shallow-water areas close to land and ice, completely encircling the polar basin. Two separate and separated subspecies, or races, are recognized. Those of Round Island are the Pacific subspecies, *Odobenus rosmarus divergens*. The Atlantic subspecies, which we photographed on an island north of Hudson Bay in 1976, is *O. r. rosmarus*. The generic name *Odobenus* means "tooth walker" and of course refers to the tusks that are the unique characteristics. These tusks, which are actually elongated upper canine teeth of pure ivory, are present in both males and females. The principal difference between Atlantic and Pacific walruses is in the Pacific's longer tusks and larger body size. Also, far more Pacific than Atlantic walruses survive now. The total Pacific population is estimated at about 75,000–80,000 animals—again about 10,000 of which are mature bulls.

Basically seallike in body form, walruses have flexible hind flippers that can be rotated forward; thick, heavy necks; and broad muzzles, from which many short, stiff bristles grow. Females may reach a ton in weight, or half that of an adult male. Mature bulls are recognized by the larger bulk, broader muzzles, heavier tusks, and the numerous large tubercles on necks and shoulders.

Pacific walruses are migratory, the herds of females, called cows, moving back and forth seasonally with the advance and retreat of sea ice—southward in winter, then north in summer. In the Alaskan portion of the Bering and Chukchi seas, Bristol Bay and Point Barrow are the approximate southern and northern limits of travel. The Round Island bulls probably remain in that general area most of the time, joining the female herds in the wintering areas, usually in late December or January. Mating takes place in February or March with cows six or seven years or older. Because of delayed implantation, probably common to all pinnipeds, the fetus does not begin to grow until

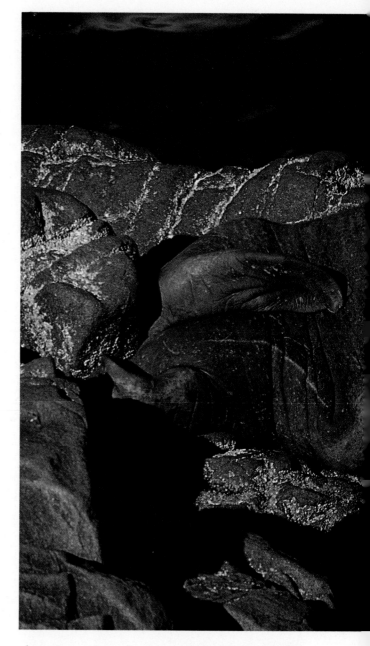

about June when the main female herd is farthest north. So although the total gestation period is a long 13 months, the actual fetal growth period is 10 months long. Birth takes place during migration in late April or May. New calves weigh 85 to 140 pounds and are dependent on their mothers for between 18 months to 2½ years. Therefore cows do not breed again until at least the year following the birth of the last calf, or even less frequently as they age.

The age of any walrus can be determined with some accuracy from the number of rings or annual layers counted in cross sections of the teeth. In very old individuals, some of the earliest, outer, growth rings may be worn away with use. But the examination of

Bachelor bulls lead lives of comparative indolence, basking, bathing, mostly resting, going to sea occasionally to feed.

many teeth has revealed that the Pacific subspecies can potentially reach 35 years of age. Bulls continue to grow for the first 14 or 15 years of their lives and perhaps longer. But not many of either sex die of old age, as I will explain later in this chapter.

To reach their great size, walruses depend on the abundance of bottom-dwelling invertebrates that thrive on the relatively shallow and rich Bering-Chukchi Platform. Several varieties of clams are the major foods. But only the protruding parts are usually eaten, the "foot" of some species, or the siphons of others. Probably these desirable parts are torn away from the rest of the clam by strong suction that is possible because a walrus' mouth is perfectly designed

for this strange method of feeding. Walruses locate clams by sweeping the sea bed with their broad, flat muzzles.

Notice in the accompanying photos how the mouth is narrow with an unusually high roof and strong, thick lips for sucking in. These thick lips are not deeply cleft, so the gape is quite limited. Walruses also have heavy, pistonlike tongues that are probably not used very much in feeding. Walruses are known to catch

Left: Much fighting, some seemingly serious and some not, takes place in shallow
water around bull walrus haulout points. At this spot, I watched bulls sparring with
ivory tusks for hours. Above: Walruses are highly gregarious. This offshore rock was
vacated when our boat came too close. Soon the rock was again full to capacity.

and eat the pups of fur seals and sea lions when these
first begin to swim. The only natural enemies of walruses are orcas—killer whales—and on rare occasions
in the winter, polar bears.

Much speculation has been published on the purpose of walrus tusks. They might be used to pry stub-
born invertebrates from the sea bottom. Today, most
scientists believe that the species moves head down,
in an almost vertical position, along the seabed in
from 30- to 150-foot depths. They may glide along
using the tusks like sled runners. Clams are routed by
the upper edge of the snout, not by the tusks. Male
tusks are often used in mutual display. The stronger
animals usually have the larger tusks and they are
usually dominant over bulls with smaller tusks. I have
seen the bulls use tusks when sparring both on land
and in water, but the bouts were usually brief and did
not seem deadly serious.

When walruses are disturbed on a Round Island
beach or when resting on an ice floe, which happens
frequently, they respond by raising heads high to display the tusks. Individuals with smaller ivory usually

move a short distance away (if there is room), or at
least become respectfully quiet. But observers who
have studied Pacific walruses throughout their life
cycle have reported occasional violent battles between
bulls with about the same body and tusk dimensions.
The males I have seen on Round Island do not bear
nearly the great number of scars and open wounds as
do the fur seals and sea lion bulls we have seen elsewhere in Alaska.

Another possible reason for tusks is their utilitarian
value as levers to help the animals pull themselves
out onto ice shelves or steep, rocky beaches. They
might also have emergency uses. Biologist John J.
Burns once watched a cow literally demolish a chunk
of ice to free her calf, which had rolled into a crevasse.
The tusks proved as effective as a pickax, and the
presence of a dozen men only 30 feet away did not
distract the female walrus from her mission. When
the men attempted to help rescue the 100-pound calf,
according to Burns, "the cow charged them furiously,
with a threatening noise made as she opened and
closed her mouth, the noise sounding much like a

Left: Round Island is a breeding island for arctic seabirds, especially for murres and
black-legged kittiwakes, which occupy even the narrowest ledges on this rock cliff.
Above: Glaucous-winged gulls swarm over the waters off Togiak, feeding on the offal
from salmon canneries.

man banging a sewer pipe with a hammer. So we returned to our own tasks, and in due time she freed
her calf and swam away, carrying it on her back."

Although a Pacific walrus of any size is a formidable
animal, walruses are not really difficult to hunt, especially with modern firearms, seaworthy boats, and
motorized vessels. Traditionally the species was a
mainstay in many Alaskan Eskimo villages along the
Bering Sea. The meat was important for food, the
skins covered Eskimo boats, and the intestines were
crafted into raingear almost as effective as modern
plastics. The tusks were carved into useful tools and
also fashioned as souvenirs and sold "outside." But
although dependence on walruses has all but vanished
in the late 1980s, the hunting continues, less out of
need than habit.

Villagers around the Bering Strait, Gambell, Sa-
voonga, King Island, and Little Diomede Island harvest between 1,500 and 2,000 animals every year. Siberian Eskimos also take a good many more. But these
totals are deceptive because at least one and almost
certainly several are wounded and lost for each one
retrieved and counted as a kill. One biologist-observer,
who asked to remain anonymous, told me that during

one village hunt he monitored, 11 walruses were hit
by rifle fire, but only 2 were retrieved and brought to
shore. Considering that the Pacific population seems
to be in a steady decline, the time has probably come
to phase out walrus hunting permanently.

Wisely, the Walrus Islands State Game Sanctuary
was set aside in 1960, providing an unequaled opportunity to see and study such an extraordinary concentration of the animals, and the last hauling-out
grounds in the southern Bering Sea. The sanctuary
includes seven islands, but Round is the largest and
most important.

After our first evening of photographing the bulls
in warm, late afternoon sunlight, we hiked outward
to other points on the island. On the southern tip
we found a rookery of Steller's sea lions, but they were
much warier than the walruses. On another trek, and
while we were still some distance from the top of a
tall sea cliff, the din of thousands of screaming seabirds
became louder and louder until we came directly opposite the cliff on which common murres, black-legged
kittiwakes, and puffins were nesting. As we had on
such nesting cliffs elsewhere, we watched an almost
bewildering spectacle.

While some birds were launching outward from the cliffs on fishing expeditions (some flying as far as, or even farther away than, the Togiak cannery on the mainland), other birds were constantly returning, refueled, to feed the young birds that crouched waiting on narrow ledges. Not all calculated their landings accurately; we witnessed more than a few missed approaches and even crash landings into perched birds. The result was usually a noisy squabble throughout the immediate "neighborhood."

While watching the seabird spectacle, we were joined by Judy Sherburne, who for the second summer

Peace reigns on Alaska's "Ivory Coast." Used in display and fighting, tusks also serve like sled runners as walruses swim along sea bottom. Tusks also serve as tools to help their owners onto beaches and ice floes—and even as ice picks.

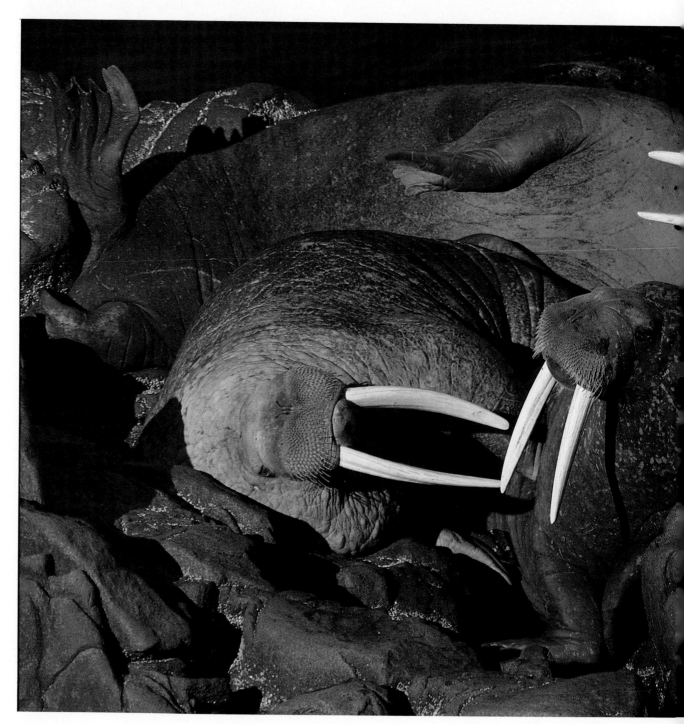

was serving as the Alaska Department of Fish & Game's biologist-caretaker of Round Island. Because the number of visitors is limited (a free permit from ADF&G is necessary), and because poaching for walrus ivory has been too tempting at times in the past, an official human presence is necessary.

For a number of summers, Alaska biologists, also husband and wife, Jim Taggary and Cindy Zabel shared the damp, lonely, and isolated three-month

management post, which required a great dedication to wilderness and wild creatures. They lived in the single, tiny but snug frame shack, which was cabled to earth against wind on an open slope.

Judy Sherburne, who lives there now with her biologist husband Bob Lipchak, is equally dedicated and had married Bob only two weeks before we arrived. The service was solemnized on a Round Island cliff overlooking the Bering Sea by the captain of the research vessel *Rainier* of the National Oceanic and Atmospheric Administration which happened to be passing. Don Winkleman and other wedding guests had to race back to Togiak immediately after the outdoor ceremony as predictions of a fast-approaching storm crackled over all marine radios in the Bristol Bay area. Round Island became completely socked in, lashed by 60-knot gales and heaving seas for several days after the nuptials. This may be the most tempestuous honeymoon island on the planet.

In bright sunlight the carcasses of bull walruses sprawled along the beach had a bright rosy or reddish color, and, in fact, except for the pure white tusks, the beach seemed to be a mass of red shades. But while chatting with Sherburne, we noticed that a few of the bulls nearest the water's edge were of a sharply contrasting, pale lavender color. Even as we watched, another lilac bull swam almost leisurely toward land and out onto bare rocks. I wondered about the color variation.

Sherburne explained. When walruses are forced to dive deep to feed, and to stay down very long in the cold water, oxygen-rich blood, which is normally near the skin surface, retreats to maintain the vital internal organs: the heart, kidneys, and brain. This extends the animal's foraging time, but the migration of blood causes the ruddy hue to fade. After the walrus returns to the surface and hauls out, the reoxygenated blood slowly returns to the skin. I watched as an almost gray creature near me turned first to a pale pink, then warmed to its usual color, which is rose in the heat of the sun.

Back in camp that evening, broiling salmon steaks over hickory charcoal (toted all the way from Tennessee via Anchorage), we kept conversation entirely to the incredible combination of perfect weather and a shoreline that was wall-to-wall walrus. That's when we met another of Round Island's residents, this one, like us, an alien. A thin red fox simply materialized at the edge of our group and stared curiously at all, lingered a little longer to scratch, and then climbed onto an exposed rock nearby where it could watch us, one eye partly opened, while curled up half asleep. After that we saw it often.

Early in this century when fox fur was in great de-

Above: Ancestors of this red fox were stocked on Round Island early in the 20th century by "fur farmers" looking for an easy way to feed and confine them. Seabirds became the food, and the sea served as the fence. Top right: Ponderous and lethargic as they may seem, bull walruses can be wary and nervous. A subtle warning, even a loose rock rolling down a cliff, can send a whole herd into the sea. Bottom right: More sparring.

mand worldwide and the value of fox pelts was high, a good many Alaskans got into fox farming the easy way. Instead of building elaborate pens and raising the animals in captivity, they simply released pairs of animals (both reds and arctic foxes) indiscriminately on hundreds of offshore islands from Ketchikan in the extreme southeast and throughout the Aleutian Islands. They figured correctly that thriving on the bounty of nesting seabirds, on small native rodents, and on carrion that washed ashore, the released foxes would prosper and multiply in their isolation, unable to escape. The surplus then could be easily harvested annually when the pelts were prime. No labor, no capital investment, no feed bills. Only profit.

The scheme worked in many places, but to the great detriment of nesting bird populations, which were even eliminated in some places. The total damage has been hard to measure. Fortunately the steep cliffs on Round and many other islands have limited the possible predation, as well as the fox numbers. On Round the fox population still fluctuates greatly from

10 or fewer to many times that number from one year to the next. But no matter what the number, we encountered them often and found that they were never shy of the few humans that appeared on the island.

It was difficult not to keep hiking back to the same overlooks to watch the splendid marine mammals that are rarely observed at close range anywhere else in the world. From a distance a beach full of bulls seems to be a fairly peaceful scene of living the bachelor idyll. But on closer inspection, it is not so calm. There is always a section of the mass that seethes with annoyance. Each time one bull moves, either to head for the water or to return, it sets up a ripple effect of grunting, bellowing, blowing, tusk raising. Here and there the jostling escalates into angry disputes for space or right-of-way. A newcomer back from foraging at sea is not warmly greeted, but once settled in, bulky sides pressed against its neighbors, it becomes one of the group and then resents any others who insist on joining the club. Only the largest old tuskers find a resting place without too much trouble.

Watching any of the 1½-ton giants climb out of the water and up onto sometimes steep rocks gives a good appreciation of both the animal's power and its awkwardness on land. The bull hunches forward on its front flippers to support part of its massive weight, then immediately arches its back to swing the rear end forward. Finally the rear flippers swing ahead to keep up with the rest of the body, and the whole process is repeated. But this clumsiness on land is compensated by impressive agility, speed, even grace once a walrus is back in the water.

At intervals on some invisible signal, perhaps a perceived danger, all the bulls in an area will suddenly stampede toward the water by the shortest possible route. The result is total confusion, and for a while the beach may remain cleared. Or the bulls might return immediately. I wondered why the males re-

After a walrus returns from a long, deep dive its skin changes color from gray-lavender to pink and then rose as reoxygenated blood gradually returns to the skin surface.

mained separated so long from the females and concluded that it is a natural way to disperse the population and not deplete food supplies in any one place.

On our last scheduled night on the island I sat through the long, yellow twilight on a cliff about 100 feet above the surf to watch, listen, and savor what probably would be my last time ever on Round Island. Bulls were trading places, back and forth parallel to the rocky shore, sometimes blowing and splashing. Especially I noticed two bulls not far from water's edge, floating vertically like humans treading water, facing

each other. Then for five minutes or more, when the soft breeze that swirled below was just right, I could hear the belling, the chimes, that came from the same air sacs that give the bulls their buoyancy. At that time in that place, the sound seemed totally unreal.

Next morning, as soon as we could see the *Puffin II* on the horizon, heading our way from Togiak, we struck tents, folded tripods, and began the slow task of lugging our gear back down to the beach.

By noon the boat was anchored just offshore in a gradually increasing chop. Our party and paraphernalia were carefully ferried out from shore. The two-hour ride back to Togiak through skeins of murres and guillemots skimming low over the swells was rougher than the trip outward. The last good look we had at Round, the mysterious, treeless island with the single 1,400-foot spine in the center, was from 14 miles away. Round Island was quickly vanishing beneath the clouds of a Bering Sea summer.

It is hard to overstate our extremely good fortune in having had solid sunshine during our stay. For the next 10 days the climatic conditions were more usual for the place. A severe and sometimes savage storm blasted the sanctuary, and the next party to visit was trapped inside their tents by winds that made just standing up outside difficult.

So I have good advice for anyone who plans to visit Round in the future. The island certainly is one of the matchless treasures of wild Alaska, but a traveler should go well prepared. Carry along everything needed for a siege of vicious weather. That includes a tough tent, rated for the worst gales with all stakes firmly rooted. Also take ample food and a warm sleeping bag, plus clothing that includes durable foul-weather suits and hip-high waterproof boots for hiking through tall grass that may be soaking wet even on the nicer days. Also bring every possible protection for photographic equipment and film.

Summed up, Round Island is an extraordinary place, not to be taken lightly, but not to be missed.

CHAPTER SEVEN
Best Fishing in America

Look straight down," Bob Curtis shouted above the roar of the floatplane's motor. Then he pointed and banked the craft to give me a better view of the tundra.

In a shallow, reedy oxbow, two moose had been standing unconcerned and belly-deep in the water 800 feet below us. But when the shadow of the plane brushed too close to the animals, they galloped toward the nearest timber. I grabbed a camera to photograph them, but it was too late. A mile farther on, Bob cut back on the throttle and began a wide, sweeping circle. He pointed to a double-S-shaped bend below where the Nuyakuk River raced through a sheer rocky canyon, finally pouring over a falls. This was an absolutely magnificent, primeval scene.

"We'll land in the big pool just below the falls," our pilot said.

Several moments later we skimmed across the surface and taxied close to a gravel shore. When Bob cut the motor, I jumped off the pontoon with the anchor rope and lashed it to the stoutest willow nearby. Peggy and I then hurried to set up our tackle with unsteady hands. The river before us was enough to excite anyone.

I rigged my fly rod and made the first cast into water almost as transparent as the atmosphere. I made an inaccurate delivery and forgot about retrieving my fly when I saw what followed. The river was alive with the dark forms of grayling, startled by the line falling into the water. There must have been a dozen of them, and some were large.

Suddenly my line straightened out, and the fly rod was dancing. A grayling catapulted out of the water— once, twice, and a third time—before I could shout "Strike!" Next thing I knew another grayling was leaping, this one on the end of Peggy's line. We managed to land them both.

Above: Fishing on the Alaska Peninsula one day, I startled this cow moose filling up on aquatic vegetation. Previous page: Much of Alaska's best sport-fishing is accessible by floatplane. Peggy hooked this rainbow on such a trip.

The rest of our morning on the Nuyakuk was a never-to-be-forgotten story of fast action with a great gamefish. Almost wherever they are found in the far North, grayling are willing strikers and great jumpers, and these were no exception. Not many of our casts, with either small flies or tiny spinners, went untouched. But the most exciting incident that morning had nothing to do with grayling.

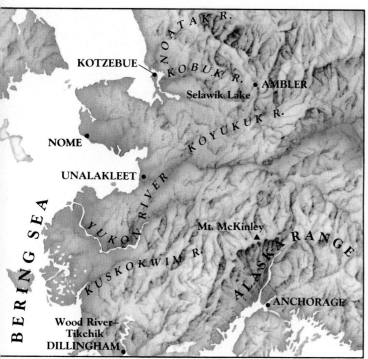

SELECTED SITES FROM THIS CHAPTER

I first fished the region in 1971 with Bob as my guide. He's a former bush-mail pilot, who had explored every remote corner of Alaska and later became a noted big-game outfitter. He selected Wood-Tikchik as the best area for sport fishing, and with his wife, Gayle, built a modest fishing camp at Tikchik Narrows, beside the thin, rocky channel that separates Nuyakuk from Tikchik Lake. It's a scenic spot, and I can recall catching both lakers and rainbows from a raft anchored just outside the door of Bob's camp. On that same trip we had also caught eight different species of fish within an hour's flight by floatplane from the Narrows camp. It was the best freshwater fishing trip I'd ever taken.

Bob had invited us to fish with him again, and his camp was now expanded to accommodate 12 anglers. It had all the amenities you could expect to find in a quality accommodation much closer to civilization. "The fishing is just as good as you remember it," Bob had written us in a winter letter. So we headed back for Tikchik during a trip to Alaska early in 1974.

I had waded upstream to where the froth of the falls dissolved into a smooth, swift glide and managed to drop a colorful streamer fly right in that spot with a double-haul cast. I began a slow, hand-twist retrieve, allowing the loops of line to fall on the water at my feet. Just as I was ready to pick up and cast again, I saw a huge rainbow trout coming up fast behind the fly. I'm still not certain what happened next. Maybe the trout made a lightning pass at the fly and missed. Maybe I struck too soon and took the fly away. Maybe something else. But the rainbow continued closer in slower motion until he was less than 10 feet from where I stood. He regarded me for a split second and then darted out of sight. I'm convinced that he was among the largest trout (other than a laker) I've ever seen alive. And no amount of diligent casting, changing of flies, or special techniques was enough to raise that monster fish again.

WOOD RIVER–TIKCHIK LAKES COUNTRY.

The action took place in June in the southwestern part of Alaska usually known as the Wood River–Tikchik Lakes country. The area is 350 air miles west of Anchorage and just north Dillingham (population 417). It's a lonely, lovely land of mountains and muskeg flats mixed with interlocking lakes and drained by a number of clean, free-flowing rivers. The Wood-Tikchik country is a spectacularly beautiful area in a state that abounds in breathtaking scenery. According to Bob Curtis, Wood-Tikchik contains the best fishing in Alaska, but of course he's prejudiced.

An old fishing friend, John Moxley, holds his catch of Arctic char in the Wood River–Tikchik area. That's Bob Curtis with the paddle.

A sockeye salmon fresh from the ocean is about the finest game and table species of all Alaskan fishes. This one came from Chenik Creek.

It's a comfortable 3½-hour flight from Seattle to Anchorage, 90 minutes more to Dillingham, and about an hour by Grumman Goose from Dillingham to the doorstep of Tikchik Narrows. The afternoon of our arrival we caught Dolly Varden trout and sockeye salmon in the Togiak River, just over the Wood River Mountains west of Bob's lodge.

No matter when or where you headquarter in Alaska, bad weather—at least very damp and dreary weather—eventually is a factor to consider. We always take clothing that is suitable for both warm and cold temperatures, and especially for rain. Throughout the day following our arrival, we were trapped indoors by a steady cold downpour, which stopped only very late during the long arctic twilight.

The next morning our fly-out-by-floatplane destination was a featureless lake of the Togiak drainage, nameless on all available charts but remarkable nonetheless. It lay in a shallow, treeless basin and was surrounded by a network of bear trails etched deep into the earth. The paths converged like spokes of a wheel at the inlet and outlet of the lake. That's where the fish were concentrated, and we could see their dark forms in the water as we approached for a landing.

The easiest to catch were the Dolly Vardens, locally called char. Varying greatly in color from spotted pewter to pale pink, and with white-edged fins, the Dollies ran from 13 to about 18 inches. The biggest fish in those waters were the red, or sockeye, salmon fresh from the sea, still silvery in color, that ran up to 10 pounds or a bit more.

Sockeyes are unpredictable. In some places they readily strike artificial lures during their freshwater spawning runs. In the famous Brooks River of Alaska's Katmai National Park, they even take streamer flies, at times avidly. But elsewhere the reds strike at nothing and are caught on rod and reel only by snagging, which is legal in some river drainages. I wondered if those sockeyes would hit my lures.

The immediate answer seemed to be no. Fifteen to 20 minutes of tossing hardware with a bass plugcasting outfit produced nothing, and I began to lose interest. I considered rigging up a fly rod and wading downstream from the lake outlet to where Bob said I would find grayling and small rainbows. I was listlessly retrieving my spoon when I had a strike that I could feel down to my heels.

Before I could catch my reel handles, a silvery sockeye leaped from the water in a crazy, tarponlike jump. While the monofilament line burned my thumb on the reel spool, that salmon cleared the surface six more times before I could finally beach and release it.

Late in the afternoon Bob suggested that we soon head back to Tikchik, and I made a final cast toward a school of sockeyes that I could see cruising in the clear water. But it was a heavy rainbow trout, not one of the salmon, that peeled off and came directly toward my brass-finished lure.

Although my heart seemed to stop, I managed to keep retrieving. Just when I thought he would strike, the trout turned away and disappeared. I can still see him these many years later.

"You're rainbow-jinxed," Peggy said, "but the trip isn't over yet."

The remarkable thing about fishing in the Tikchik area is the great variety of angling. One day, for example, Cleveland sportsmen Joe Clark and Joe Siebold flew northwestward with Bob to Sleetmute, a small village on the Kuskokwim River. There they rented a boat for an upstream run on the Holitna River, where they caught sheefish. Also called inconnu, these little-known arctic relatives of the tarpon and herring readily strike spoons or plugs and reach 25 pounds or more. At the same time another party was fishing the Nushugak River, where giant king salmon were beginning to make their run up from Bristol Bay. A 28-pounder was taken on light tackle that day, but bigger ones were hooked and lost.

Because it was daylight until almost midnight, we spent some of the evening hours trolling or casting in Nuyakuk Lake for lake trout. Later we caught coho salmon over the same bars and reefs. In shallow places nearby and also later in the season, casters can take surprisingly large northern pike. In 1972 Martin Clark,

I land a lively king salmon in the Togiak River on light, freshwater bass tackle. River salmon fishing is extraordinary sport.

then maintenance supervisor of the hospital in Dillingham, caught a northern he estimated at 40 pounds. Bob Curtis claims he has seen what could be a world-record pike just a short run from his lodge. Since most visitors to Alaska would rather try for trout or salmon, so the pike fishing is almost unexploited.

On the final day of our trip we made a 15-minute shuttle to the Agulukpak River with several of the Tikchik guests: Albie Wells of Palo Alto, California; Cliff Willis, an entrepreneur from Fort Lauderdale, Florida; and Gus Pernak of Birmingham, Michigan. The Agulukpak is a 5-mile-long waterway that connects Beverley and Nerka lakes. It's big water, how-

ever, about a half mile wide where we landed near the outlet of Beverley Lake. There is more than ample space for several anglers to be fishing at one time without crowding. It's a remarkable place where grayling, rainbows, and especially Dolly Vardens are almost continuously rising and striking.

The fish catching that day could be described as nonstop. Peggy had waded out to cast, while I sat on a grassy bank to change leaders, load cameras, and keep an eye on a bear trail where the tracks looked a little too fresh. A Dolly struck on Peggy's first cast, and from then until our lunch break Peggy was busy hooking and releasing fish, some up to 4½ pounds.

Late in the afternoon Albie Wells waded wearily ashore, slumped down on the bank, and drained the last drops of coffee from a vacuum bottle. "It was my best day's fishing—ever," he said.

Whether the Wood River–Tikchik Lakes region actually offers the finest angling in Alaska or the U.S. may be impossible to determine. If you consider comparatively difficult access and the considerable cost, perhaps it doesn't compare well with other places we've fished nearer middle America. But the fish are there in quantity and great variety of species and are willing to strike. And we have never fished amid such stupendous wilderness landscapes.

We enjoyed extraordinary fishing during our stay, but my jinx continued. I had drifted a streamer fly across and downstream through a smooth run on the Agulukpak. Halfway through the drift the line suddenly straightened, and I raised the rod tip automatically to set the hook. A big rainbow arched out of the current and began a wild rush downstream. I played out line and followed while he jumped again, still headed in the general direction of the Bering Sea. Finally I stopped his run, headed the rainbow upstream, and had visions of landing the kind of trout I'd missed twice before.

I slowly reduced the distance between us and even

For my money the most exciting, premier game species in all Alaska is the silver, or coho, salmon fresh from salt water. Most coho runs occur late in summer or early in fall.

managed to retrieve all the backing, and fly line appeared inside the rod tip. Peggy stood by with a camera. A net hung handily from my vest. That's when the fish rolled to the top again, tried to jump clear, but only wallowed in the water. Such a maneuver always gives me a cold chill, and it did this time. That's when the line went slack.

I muttered, "I guess it wasn't in the cards for me to catch a trophy-room rainbow."

Peggy replied, "But what a wonderful excuse you have to come back."

THE ELUSIVE SHEEFISH. No place I have ever fished has kept calling me back the way Alaska always has. This siren song has taken me to strange places— fishing holes galore. One of the most memorable was several hundred miles north of Tikchik Lakes where a wilderness river flows almost leisurely toward the Bering Sea. I remember one indelible day there.

Arthur Douglas allowed his long, homemade skiff to drift downstream until he felt the bottom of the Kobuk River fall away. Then the young Eskimo dropped a stone anchor, played out line, and when the anchor caught, knotted the line to the gunwale. No modern technology needed there.

"We try here," Arthur said. Then he picked up an antique rod and reel and began casting a spoon he had hammered from the lid of a rusty gasoline drum. "Shees swim round this deep place at nights," he explained.

An angler might spend a lifetime fishing and never savor a scene or a situation exactly like this one. It was night, almost midnight in fact, but it wasn't dark. Instead, a strange clinging twilight illuminated the lonely arctic barrens all around. The scarlet sun ball still hovered above the horizon and Siberia. And even though this wide bend of the Kobuk was located almost a hundred miles above the Arctic Circle, the night was as warm as any summer night in Wyoming where I live.

Stranger even than the midnight twilight was the river itself. Generally shallow, milky, and slow moving, it seemed more a river of molten copper than of water as it flowed toward the setting sun and the Arctic Ocean. The river ran quietly, too, and except for the mosquitos that whined around our ears, the twilight was silent.

My son Bob and I rigged a pair of spinning rods and soon were following Arthur's example of casting cross-current and retrieving spoons as they drifted downstream. After 15 minutes of casting produced nothing, I changed spoons and was prepared to change a second time when Arthur suddenly pointed downstream. "Big shees!"

131

They were big somethings, sure enough. And there was a whole school of them. Backlit by the sunset, the school's wake was easy to follow as the fish traveled a wavering path upstream and directly toward our anchored skiff. This was a thrilling sight and made me think of the tarpon I'd seen migrating up tropical rivers thousands of miles away. As the fish came closer, I also had a touch of buck fever.

We watched and waited until the fish were within easy casting distance and then dropped three spoons just ahead of them. Instantly the lead fish turned, followed my spoon, and rolled as it struck just under the surface. A huge tail broke water and then bedlam. The instant I set the hooks, the rest of the school flushed in all directions, actually rocking the boat.

"My first shee," I said, half out loud. At least that's what Bob said I said later on.

For 10 minutes and maybe more I applied all the pressure 8 pounds of monofilament would stand as the fish made strong rushes upstream. Occasionally it would wallow on the surface and once I had to walk the length of the skiff and poke the rod tip underwater to keep it from fouling in the anchor rope. Then somehow Arthur made a quick pass with a short gaff and swung the fish, still full of fight, aboard.

Only the fish wasn't a sheefish at all. Instead it was a 12-pound, hook-jawed, male dog salmon.

"My first shee," I laughed. But I really didn't *feel* like laughing.

There's no good reason to be disappointed about catching a dog salmon, and Arthur couldn't have been happier. Dogs are powerful, good jumpers, and good on the table. But Bob and I hadn't traveled completely across a continent to this lonely place for salmon. Our target here on top of Alaska was the sheefish, or inconnu, a rare gamefish that very few anglers know well.

At the time, Bob and I had already spent a month vagabonding in Alaska, from Juneau and Admiralty Island northward to Mt. McKinley. We'd enjoyed the trip between points by car ferry, had sampled the superlative salmon fishing in a number of places, and were about ready to go home. That's when we were lucky enough, or unlucky enough, to meet Don Strode. Don was an expatriate Ohioan and a biologist with the Alaska Department of Fish & Game. Because absolutely nobody liked to hunt and fish any more than Don, he had found paradise in Alaska.

"The shees should be moving up around Kotzebue," Don had pointed out one evening. "You shouldn't leave Alaska without trying them."

At sunset we cruise Nuyakuk Lake in search of rising trout. This is an exquisite time of day.

That did it. I had heard about the mysterious sheefish, and Don just happened to have an airline schedule. There was a daily flight to Kotzebue from Anchorage, stopping at Nome en route, and Kotzebue is the closest community to sheefish country.

Situated as it is in the lonely northwestern corner of Alaska, regular air service to Kotzebue didn't seem logical at all. It was a small Eskimo village and nothing more. But summertime tourists in large numbers like to visit the Alaskan natives in their own environment—and outdoorsmen have the tourists to thank for the reasonable round-trip air fare to good sheefishing. However, too few fishermen took advantage of it then, and few do today.

On a clear day it is a doubly interesting flight. You climb high above the Alaska Range and pass within view of Mt. McKinley, the highest point in North America. Then you stop briefly at Unalakleet and Nome, both picturesque villages on the bleak shore of the Bering Sea. But Kotzebue can appear even more bleak if you do not relish barren arctic landscapes. When you step down from the plane, you know you are deep in a treeless world.

In Kotzebue we looked up Nelson "Coo-coo-gakk" Walker, who was then owner of a two-plane air-taxi service. In winter he had guided polar bear hunters on the Arctic ice pack and at other times flew Fish & Game Department biologists on aerial game surveys of the Brooks Range and points north. Not many pilots then knew the Kotzebue region more intimately, or were more willing to admit it.

"I can take you to Selawik Lake and the Selawik River," Walker said, "and you can catch shees 'til you're dizzy. But right now they're running small; 5 pounds is a big one. Or we can buzz a hundred miles up the Kobuk to Kiana or Ambler where the sheefish are big. I've seen 'em weighing 70 to 80 pounds. But catching them isn't easy."

"Let's go for the big busters," Bob said.

The flight from Kotzebue to Ambler was as remarkable as the midnight sun. From takeoff to touchdown Walker gave a running commentary on everything from the sex life of the Eskimos to what is wrong with Social Security (the answer was plenty). Kotzebue Eskimos called him Talkie Walkie, and that's easy to understand. Every time he saw a moose or bear on the ground below, and there were plenty of moose, he would stand the Cessna 180 on its nose and zoom down for a ground-level look, with commentary.

"Good practice for when we run caribou surveys," he explained.

It was also good practice for landing at Ambler because the airstrip there was only a thin gravel bar in

To fish for inconnu—sheefish—son Bob and I flew to an Indian village on the Kobuk
River. We pitched our tent where racks of salmon were drying in the sun.

the middle of the Kobuk River. Except in midsummer, it's submerged under a couple of feet of water. We had no sooner bounced to a stop in a giant cloud of dust when dozens of Eskimos came paddling over to the gravel bar from their village on the opposite bank. Among them was Arthur Douglas, whose skiff differed from the rest in that it was powered by a new Johnson outboard motor rather than by elbow grease.

"Welcome," Arthur said with a smile as wide as his face. It turned out that he was Ambler (population: 71) mayor, postmaster, welfare agent, manager of a jade-mining project, and the chief fishing guide.

"How's the guiding business?" I asked.

"It's good," he answered. "But no outside fishermen have come here since four years ago. Maybe five."

After Walker vanished back into the wild blue yonder, there was much competition among the Eskimo children to hustle our duffel into the skiffs and then over to a campsite in the village. While virtually all the villagers watched, we pitched our tent among racks of drying sheefish and teams of malemutes staked out for the summer. The dogs did not appear too friendly, and in fact Arthur's wife was at that moment in the hospital in Kotzebue recovering from an act of unfriendliness, to wit, toothprints on her behind.

But, oh, the racks of drying sheefish! They contained none of the 70- or 80-pounders Walker had mentioned, but few of the fish would have weighed less than 20 pounds when fresh. We didn't even notice the overripe odor, and it looked like Ambler was a good place for a fisherman to be. But not for very long.

After dinner we loaded the tackle in Arthur's skiff and spent the evening fishing a horseshoe bend in the Kobuk about a mile from camp. But it was only exercise. About the only excitement came when a white-haired Eskimo lady paddled by to check a gill net she had placed in an eddy. She removed about 15 whitefish from the net, waved, and then paddled back to the village. Around 10 P.M. Arthur cranked up the outboard, and we traveled downstream about an hour. The place we stopped is where we caught the dog salmon.

But landing that fish was like flipping a switch or finding the right combination to a treasure. All at once the Kobuk came alive. Bob made a random cast across current and had barely started his retrieve when he had a soft strike. It was so soft he wasn't sure it was a strike at all, but raised his rod tip sharply anyway. That stung the fish, and it turned into the current.

"Probably another salmon," Bob said.

Bob tightened the drag slightly on his spinning reel, and far below us the fish lurched out of the water. Then, changing directions, it half jumped again, and Bob gained a little line.

"This one a shee," Arthur promised.

"You shouldn't have said it," Bob replied, "because now I'm nervous."

Nervous or not, he handled the fish skillfully. When it turned upstream, directly toward the boat, he felt he'd lost it but reeled quickly to take up slack line just in case. That was a good move because next the fish wallowed on top and minutes later it was thumping on the bottom of the boat. The shee weighed only 4 or 5 pounds and was the smallest taken in three days of fishing. But that didn't keep Bob from being the happiest young man in the 49th state. He had come far to enjoy the rare catch.

Maybe six casts later it was my turn. I had the same deceiving soft strike, but in the next instant almost had the rod torn from my hand. I didn't have to set the hooks. All I could do was hold on.

"Be ready to pull up the anchor," I said to Arthur. As nearly as I could tell in the dim light, his face was one wide grin.

The fish made a wide circle across the current, and we could easily follow the wake it made through very shallow water. But abruptly it turned downstream into the main river channel, and the way line peeled from the reel, I figured it a cinch to reach Siberia. More line evaporated from the reel, and I wondered how much was left.

"Lift the anchor," I said anxiously.

The duel that followed will not be easy to forget. I'd come a long way to catch the fish now on my line and which kept boring toward the bottom. Probably that made me more cautious than I needed to be. It seemed my reel would run out of line before the shee ran out of gas. But things began to improve when Arthur lifted the stone anchor and we were able to follow downstream.

It's hard to say how much time elapsed in bringing the shee to the boat. Five or six minutes, I suspect. But eventually the big fish was wallowing nearby. There I could see it was actually longer than my arm, and to make matters worse, Arthur had only stung the critter with his first pass of the gaff, causing it to explode partially out of the water. Fortunately that was all. On the second try, Arthur gaffed the fish and muscled it into the boat. I slumped down to admire the 20-pound fish as the hook fell out of its mouth.

The first thing a fisherman notices about a sheefish is its more than superficial resemblance to a tarpon. Although it has little scientific relationship to the tarpon, there is great similarity in its general shape, its silvery color, and the characteristic underslung lower jaw. Smaller shees, like tarpon, are also very acrobatic.

That night one fish was lost, six were landed, and together these would have weighed more than 100 pounds. Wearily, when heavy mists began to enshroud the river and action came to a sudden halt, Arthur again cranked up the outboard and we hurried back to Ambler. We arrived at 3:00 A.M. and rolled into bed. Already the sun was well up in the sky and beginning to dissolve the mist.

The sheefish is the most predaceous member of the worldwide whitefish family. It lives in an isolated, limited, and still-undefined range that includes several river systems in Alaska and corresponding latitudes across the Chukchi Sea in Asia. It regularly commutes between brackish water near the sea to fresh waters inland, sometimes as far as 1,000 miles inland.

Shees are possibly more abundant in the Kobuk than anywhere else. At least they are caught here in greater numbers because Eskimos fish more intensively here. Shees have been found in smaller numbers in the Yukon and Kuskokwim Rivers, as well as in the Noatak and Koyukuk river drainages. A nonmigratory or landlocked population is said to exist in Great Slave Lake, Canada, but little if anything is known about it. Except for dog salmon and perhaps in a few places with arctic char, shees do not share their waters with any other gamefish.

At midmorning, a circle of Eskimo children had gathered around our tent. Already they had dressed out the shees, had tossed the entrails to the dogs, and were building tiny smokey fires of willow beneath the split carcasses placed on drying racks. When I poked my head out of the tent, most of them scattered. Maybe they were startled to see such red color in anybody's eyes—we hadn't had too much sleep.

Since the Kobuk mail plane was scheduled to make its weekly visit, postmaster Douglas suggested that we take his skiff and go fishing alone. He mentioned a couple of places upstream where sheefish concentrate, and after breakfast we headed out to try them. Everybody else stayed in the village to wait for the plane.

The Kobuk is a vastly different place in bright daylight than during midsummer's long twilight. The water is surprisingly warm, and whenever the breeze dies, mosquitos in clouds venture out from the bank and become a nuisance. Even more annoying is that the sheefish quit striking altogether. Almost, that is.

We had cast several areas thoroughly without results and had moved to the pool where the Ambler River enters the Kobuk. After dropping anchor, I put aside my tackle and stretched out in the warm sunshine for a nap. Next thing I knew, Bob was up on his feet and having a hard time trying to catch his reel handles. Fifty feet away a huge, silvery shee rolled to the surface, waved its tail, and snapped an 8-pound line as easily as a piece of string.

Bob was crushed. For the next hour both of us lashed that section of the river with a great variety of lures. But it was wasted effort.

If anything, the second evening was a photocopy of the first. With his postal duties finished, Arthur joined us again, and once the action began, we had a satisfyingly busy time at the downstream pool. On one occasion we had three fish hooked at once, although only one was boated in all the confusion. Another rubbed off the lure against the outboard propeller, and a third simply snapped the line on his way back to Kotzebue. Altogether we landed five, and a 17- or 18-pounder was the smallest.

We had one more night to fish before Coo-coo-gakk Walker was scheduled to return to pick us up, so we determined to fish hard and make the most of it. Two other skiffs of Eskimos joined us at the same place where we'd had the most luck before. Watching them fish was almost as interesting as fishing, ourselves.

About 11 P.M. the first shee was hooked by one of the Eskimos nearby. When the fish struck his spoon

he set the hook almost hard enough to turn the critter inside out. Then he stood up and reeled for all he was worth. Almost instantly the fish was flopping in the boat, and there the fisherman attacked it vigorously with a club. When the flopping ceased he picked up rod and reel without ceremony or comment and began casting again.

My big opportunity came well after midnight, after I had begun to yawn and feel the creeping chill of the arctic half-light. We had four good fish in the boat and that seemed like enough. One of the Eskimo skiffs headed back for the village, and then another followed. I kept casting, but my line was listless. Bob changed lures and rubbed his hands together to warm

Bob Bauer lands a heavy sheefish on the Kobuk River in northwestern Alaska. Not many anglers know this species.

them. At that moment I felt the soft, almost uncertain tug on my line. Automatically I raised the rod tip to set the hooks and immediately I had my hands full.

What followed wasn't a wild and violent fight. Rather the fish cut leisurely into the current and then headed downstream. It was in no hurry and it never came to the top. It swam away without pause as if not hooked at all, while line steadily moved from under my hand to the water.

"We've got to follow this one," I shouted.

Arthur tried to free the anchor, but it had caught solidly on the bottom and he had to fumble with it for several minutes. That delay was too much. With a long belly of line in the current far downstream, I

tightened the drag on the reel and the line snapped. I almost snapped, too.

For a short time I felt a little sick, a little angry. That had been a jumbo fish. But as I reached into my tackle box for more line I thought, shucks, it's a long evening; we can fish as long as our strength lasts. I noticed, too, that Bob was fishing with renewed interest, for who could tell but what the biggest shees in the river were moving in on us.

I slapped a mosquito and watched a wedge of ducks fly by. Then I braced myself and made another cast.

CHAPTER EIGHT

The Greatest Wildlife Show

July 7, 1986, was a day that did not begin auspiciously and by midmorning offered little promise of improvement. Cold and rain greeted us when we awoke in a campground outside Homer on the Kenai Peninsula. Soon after breakfast we learned that our morning charter flight with Kachemak Air Service to McNeil River State Game Sanctuary had been cancelled.

"The weather out there on the Alaska Peninsula," pilot Jose DeCreeft explained, "is thick enough to swim in. It may not clear up at all today." So we spent most of the day cleaning and recleaning our photographic equipment in a drafty tool shed where the idle Otter floatplane was moored.

But suddenly in late afternoon, the overcast at our destination had lifted, and even though rain still fell in Homer, we loaded enough camping equipment and supplies for more than a week, and DeCreeft aimed the aircraft westward over the Gulf of Alaska. Just after we passed the landmark island volcano, Augustine, mostly obscured behind clouds, we suddenly emerged into a different, sunlit world. An hour and about 100 miles after takeoff in Homer, we descended and landed softly on the shallow tidal lagoon of the McNeil River, then taxied onto a stony beach. The first thing I noted stepping ashore on that lonely wilderness was a single brown bear crossing the mud flat in the distance. Then, looking down, I noticed a pile of bear droppings on the otherwise empty beach.

A moment later one of the only two summer residents at McNeil River, biologist Larry Aumiller, appeared from nowhere to help us with our luggage. While Larry, my wife Peggy, and I backpacked the gear about a quarter of a mile to a campsite in dense,

Brown bears use many different techniques to fish—stalking, wading, waiting with extreme patience and plunging right in.

SELECTED SITES FROM THIS CHAPTER

knee-deep grass on higher ground, we heard the roar of the Otter taking off. It circled once before leaving us in one of the most incredible places in an incredible state.

At the designated public—and completely primitive—campsite, the only one within 50 miles in any direction, Aumiller suggested that we delay pitching our tent for a while and instead set up our cameras. "The chum salmon run in McNeil is just beginning," he explained, "and right now there are only a few bears fishing for them at the falls. But there are several brownies a short hike from here, and we might use this remaining sunlight to good advantage."

What followed was an evening three addicted outdoor photographers would never forget. Following a deep bear trail through iris and lupine, we soon came upon the first of the nine bears we would meet. A sow, golden in the low light of a subarctic evening, was browsing on the lush grass which had grown belly-high. Every now and then one or more of her straw-colored triplet cubs would stand erect and reveal itself nearby. All of them knew of our presence even before they saw us because the wind was blowing in their direction. But the family continued to munch grass and move about, unalarmed, as we ran roll after roll of film through three cameras.

Even when these four bears disappeared into a slough, we could keep shooting. Two hundred yards farther we met another female, this one with larger, twin 2½-year-old cubs, also eating their way toward the lowering sun. We followed them at 400mm telephoto lens distance. When the mother abruptly stood up and looked intently behind her, it was not due to concern for our presence, but instead because of the approach of a solitary male bear. This *was* a matter for concern. Like many other bruins we would encounter in the McNeil area during the coming days, this mother was more tolerant of humans than of certain other bears.

Just before sundown a raw wind began to blow, and shivering as much from the excitement as from the cold, Peggy and I turned back to set up camp before total darkness would descend. But we were barely underway when another male bear, or perhaps the same one the sow had seen before, materialized directly in our path. It seemed to study us for a long moment while standing erect on hind feet for a better view, before continuing on its way. The pictures we made of that bear looming briefly in the last glow of the setting sun at 11:30 P.M. are the most treasured among the thousands of exposures we have ever made of brown and grizzly bears. I could not fall asleep that night for thinking about that exquisite scene.

THE MCNEIL RIVER SANCTUARY. It is an understatement to write that no sanctuary on earth offers more or better opportunities to watch wild bears than the McNeil unit. It is managed wisely and very well by the Alaska Department of Fish & Game. Here is a good place to explain how it was established, for what purpose, and how it is regarded today.

The migration of chum salmon into the McNeil River has traditionally drawn populations of brown bears to the area. The fish gather in rapids and pools at the base of McNeil Falls before attempting to somehow leap them and continue their spawning journey upstream. So it is here that bears also congregate annually to gorge on the bounty. And their presence was not unknown to hunters.

Before Alaskan statehood, in a move to protect one

of the territory's largest concentrations of brown bears, the government in 1955 closed the McNeil River drainage to hunting. In 1967 the Alaska state legislature continued the hunting ban and designated about 85,000 acres of the area as a state game sanctuary. Reports vary, but as many as 670 individual bears have been counted around the falls of the McNeil River during the annual spawning run of the salmon. We

had counted as many as 50 different bears in a single day. During an earlier visit to McNeil in the late 1970s, Peggy and I recorded 36 in one afternoon. Prior to 1973 no restrictions or regulations existed for visiting the river. The result was that an increasing number of visitors arrived to see "the bear show," and camped where they pleased, often right on bear trails. Some left garbage behind and in general behaved as

As many as 670 individual brown bears have been counted around the falls of the McNeil River during the annual salmon spawning run.

unpredictably as the bears are said to behave. What happened was that the animals began to abandon the place, or came only at night, and there were the predictable bear–human incidents.

No one has studied brown bears more thoroughly than biologist Larry Aumiller, for many years the manager at McNeil River State Game Sanctuary.

During 1971 and 1972, the number of visiting bears dropped to 25 or 30, and as low as 12 per day during the peak of the salmon run. In view of this situation, the state game officials decided that strict regulations had become absolutely necessary.

Recognizing that the sanctuary's primary function was to host as many bears as would be normal if undisturbed, biologists also realized that a limited number of people could view the animals without markedly altering their activities. Just one person wandering in the vicinity of the falls could keep some bears from staying very long, or from returning to fish, and the greater the number of unregulated humans, the more bears shied away. After considerable debate it was decided that a maximum of 10 people per day would be allowed to visit the falls. Although a group of this size might originally have reduced the number of fishing bears, the bear population has gradually increased in the late 1980s to that of the 1950s.

Specifically, 10 people are permitted access to the sanctuary for a four-day period. Since there are many more people wanting access than available permits, an annual public lottery is held to determine which candidates will be awarded the permits. Peggy and I

have made an application each year, along with a minimal cash deposit, and in 15 drawings have been successful only twice.

There are other important regulations in addition to the limit in numbers. All camping is now in a single specified tenting area. (There are no accommodations or facilities whatever at McNeil. You bring along *everything* you are likely to need for a stay. There are pit toilets, a nearby spring with safe drinking water, and nothing more.) Access is by boat or charter floatplane. The camp and a small bluff overlooking McNeil Falls (about 2 miles' hike from the tentsites) where visitors watch the bears are the only two areas in the sanctuary reserved for people. Any bears that wander into or close to camp, as they sometimes do, are immediately driven away by loud boat horns. These horns are also used at the observation bluff.

LARRY AUMILLER AND THE BEARS. The bruins we have met along the McNeil River are mostly the same ones coming back year after year. Many have been given names by the several biologists who have long observed them. A few individuals have been returning for 20 years or more, and to Larry Aumiller they have become respected old friends. In fact it is impossible to write about this splendid sanctuary without describing Larry Aumiller's role.

By late summer of 1987 Aumiller had concluded 12 years as manager of the McNeil Sanctuary, never leaving his post from May (when the first eager bears arrive seeking the salmon feast) until September when the run is over and the last of the bears leave for distant hibernating areas. During that period he has spent about 176,000 hours (my estimate) watching brown-bear behavior from very close range, and almost certainly that is a record among bear biologists anywhere. Probably no one knows more about or understands the species any better.

On one July day in 1985, Aumiller counted 66 bears, weighing a total of 14 tons, within view *at one time.* That same day, he saw 90 different bears on the river between dawn and dark. Maybe the most remarkable statistic is that during his 13 years on site, between 900 and 1,000 humans have also visited McNeil. Although many of these people were unfamiliar with bears and bear behavior, some seeing a bear for the first time, there had not been a single human–bear incident. Contrast that to the "problems" in parks elsewhere.

Aumiller explains it thus: "We have 'trained' these bears to ignore people and we have tried to be as consistent as possible in everything we do. We go only to certain places, the camp area and falls viewpoint, while leaving the rest to the animals. In all interactions with bears, we act the same way every time. No surprises for the bear—and so none for us.

"I think the bears' acceptance of us is almost as interesting as that great concentration of bears itself. Through their long exposure to us, the bears know we are no threat, no competition. They're as content to let us stand in that one place at the falls and watch as they are of the gulls and ravens that swarm on the scene when the salmon are running.

"We *can* get away with strange behavior occasionally while standing above the falls, as long as nobody leaves the spot. People have sneezed, accidentally toppled tripods and cameras, have fallen from folding stools, all without a bear raising an eyebrow. But let someone step only 15 feet away to urinate, and some skittish animals nearby may bolt."

The raised location of the single observation point at McNeil is important because any people standing there are clearly visible to bears in all directions. Bears do not relish surprises, and it's wise to always let them know where you are. Equally important is that the daily trek from camp to falls and return is invariably made on exactly the same trail. This way it's possible to pass close to bears en route, usually resulting in nothing more than a sidelong glance.

As elsewhere, the brownies here are normally solitary animals. The exceptions are sows with cubs, siblings that may travel together for a year or so, and mating pairs briefly gamboling together in early summer. Typical bear behavior is to avoid one another, for lesser bears to stay clear of larger ones, even for families to avoid one another. But total avoidance is impossible during the relatively short, six-week salmon run when so many find themselves in proximity. Although getting along with other bears may be even harder (because of the competition for food) than getting along with humans, with a few exceptions the bears manage it surprisingly well. In fact I now believe that brown grizzly bears are far more adaptable than humans have thought. If the bears spent too much time quarreling in situations such as that at the McNeil River (where violent fights certainly do break out at times), they would have less time to gorge on the brief salmon bounty. Eating vast amounts during summer is vital to the survival of the bears, and time lost to fighting would be impossible to make up later.

The solution is a protocol, or fishing etiquette, or social hierarchy quickly established to permit many bears, which are normally solitary, to fish at once in a limited space. This is based on size or strength, sex,

A photographer might wander around the world and never find a place where bear photography is better than along the McNeil River.

143

and reproductive condition. The biggest, strongest bears are assured the best fishing locations. This top-ranking class includes the most powerful and, up to a point, the oldest male browns. At McNeil, some of these have virtually "owned" the same best fishing holes for many years; no other bears come near them.

Females with cubs comprise the secondary group: The older the cubs, the higher the rating within the group. Next come the siblings (twins or triplets) that are traveling together, fishing together, and throwing their weight around as a single bear. Small, unattached males and females (in that order) make up the bottom group of the McNeil hierarchy. Bears in any group normally give ground in the fishing area to bears in higher ranking groups. Most conflict occurs when bears of nearly equal size and rank come face to face, or when a new, unranked bear suddenly appears on the scene.

One morning Peggy and I had arrived at the viewing area to find a medium-size sow with twin yearling cubs at water's edge just below us on the near side of the river. Even before we could set up our cameras, a second sow, also with twin cubs of nearly the same size, arrived just downstream. From the second sow's hesitation and cautious approach I judged her to be a stranger, not quite sure of herself. But the sight of so many salmon wallowing in the cold water erased the second mother's caution, and she plunged headlong into the water in an upstream chase to catch a fish. She hadn't traveled far before she was met head-on by the first mother bear. The resulting bear bout may have been the fastest, most furious I've ever seen. The cubs, meanwhile, retreated and cowered in separate family groups.

Before we could focus on the females, the two were on hind legs biting at one another and both were bleeding around the face and shoulders. It ended when the newer arrival backed slowly away, at first giving ground, but then holding firm. Minutes after the fight had begun, both sows were fishing in a truce that kept them about 30 yards apart. The first bear remained in control of the better area, though.

Later that day, when a drizzle began and it was necessary to cover our cameras with protective plastic sacks, we had time to concentrate more on behavior than on sharp focus. The McNeil Falls site furnishes an excellent laboratory to study the way in which the animals communicate with each other. The most noticeable signals are physical, such as whether a bear approaches the site quickly and confidently, or slowly and with hesitation. When leaving, a high-ranking bear does so slowly and without ever looking back. More timid individuals hurry away, often looking back to see if anything is following. Other messages include

sidling and crouching, circling, lunging, baring teeth, standing motionless or backing up when facing a rival, or simply sitting down. Lower ranking bears may lie down and approach or pass a much larger animal on their stomachs. All these postures tend to eliminate serious conflict in a sort of live-and-let-live resolution.

Many other creatures, especially the wild dogs, use tails to send signals in body language. But since their

short tails are hidden in long hair, McNeil brown bears use heads, necks, and mouths much more to convey their intentions. Nothing indicates a bear's mood any more than the position of its head. An individual that approaches with its head above the level of its characteristic shoulder hump is neither looking for nor expecting trouble. Therefore we learned to be especially alert for, and to have our cameras aimed directly

Almost a ton of brown bear is locked in angry combat here as these males dispute a productive fishing spot. The fight ended quickly when the interloper retreated.

at, any bears that approached the salmon-fishing site with heads held low. Trouble and exciting action photos of it were likely to follow.

Triplet cubs sit huddled together, hungrily waiting for a salmon to swim close to their mother. They also watch apprehensively all around for other bears.

Late one afternoon Charlie Brown, a large male estimated to weigh well over half a ton arrived where 16 other bears were already busy pursuing salmon. Charlie strode regally to his customary fishing place. Other bruins in his path automatically gave him a wide corridor through which to pass. Twice when Charlie Brown was eating a salmon, other bears ventured a little too close, but his simply looking up to stare at them was language enough to send them away. A lesser bear might have had to open and close its mouth rapidly while salivating, or even bare its teeth and make a chomping noise to send intruders away. We noticed, though, that after Charlie Brown had eaten nine salmon, say about 75 pounds of meat, he became a little more tolerant of close approach. In fact he seemed to fall asleep while a very large, light-brown female fished only about 25 feet away.

To be quite honest every aspect of human behavior is mirrored here by the brown bears at McNeil Falls. During a typical long day when hordes of salmon in pink and greenish spawning colors are surging up from salt water to rest in cold, almost transparent pools, it is possible to witness greed (stealing salmon from smaller bears though already sated), territoriality, mother love, pretense, anger, contentment (Charlie Brown sound asleep), persistence (a small female determined to feed her cubs despite the odds), drive, covetousness, guile (one sibling distracts another's attention while the first sibling invades the second's fishing hole), competition, robbery (one cub takes another's salmon by assault), encroachment (gradually an old bear past its prime is forced out of a favorite spot), intimidation, and harassment—all of it undisguised. "It's just like life back in suburbia," Larry Aumiller once noted.

It would be hard to imagine anyone better suited to "managing," or coping so well with, the brown bears of the McNeil River than Larry Aumiller. In early middle age, he has already had a lifetime's wilderness experience with Alaskan wildlife. A native of Colorado, he served in the U.S. Army, attended college in Colorado, Kansas, and Wyoming before finding himself in Alaska and in 1972 going to work for the Alaska Department of Fish & Game.

Previous page: A passing bear tries to take a salmon from a female with cub, but is quickly driven away. Below: Low-key contests—play fights—between younger males are an almost daily occurrence at McNeil. These may be dominance or conditioning exercises more than anything else.

These two bears, probably males, met where two busy bear trails converged. The meeting triggered the scuffle that is shown in these photos, ending when one bear threw the other over onto its back.

Since then Aumiller has studied the walrus bulls of Round Island, spent a summer in the Bering Sea aboard the research vessel M/V *Kittiwake,* participated in research on king salmon, rainbow trout, and arctic grayling; and studied the huge Steller sea lion colony on uninhabited Marmot Island near Kodiak. In southeastern Alaska, Aumiller ran a moose-checking station, censused waterfowl in the Copper River delta, and captured (for transfer elsewhere) many nuisance black bears. From a tent camp on offshore ice in the Bering Sea, the biologist studied ringed and bearded seals, walrus, and beluga whales. Other summers he was engaged in everything from trapping and radio-collaring wolves, grizzly bears, and wolverines to surveying mountain goats from the air and to collecting data on Sitka blacktail deer on the ground.

Aumiller spent one winter in a subsistence life-style while trapping lynx, otter, and mink in the Wood River–Tikchik Lakes region. It would probably be impossible to cram in much more field experience than that before arriving at the McNeil River. Although his life had been exciting and challenging up to that point, nothing before matched summer life on the

McNeil River. Each day among the brown bears seemed more revealing than that before. You realize this when admiring his superb photographs and sketches.

One adventure Aumiller had not yet had when I last saw him in 1986 was to ski cross-country from the small (and closest) village of King Salmon to McNeil River. As an eagle flies, that is about 75 miles across uninhabited, undefiled mountain wilderness, mostly covered beneath deep snow until early May. Aumiller's plan was to make the trip alone in April 1986 in hopes that he might locate some dens of the bears that come to McNeil River. He figured he could positively identify most of these animals if he saw them. The trip over unfamiliar, trailless terrain would require about 10 days, for which Aumiller would have to carry every need on his back. In other words, it would be a very dangerous skiing expedition. Although volcanic ash had spewed from Augustine Island onto the snow's surface, making his plan for spring skiing too difficult in 1986, the McNeil bear man was determined to go the first springtime that conditions were favorable.

151

Early each summer, long before visitors with permits begin to arrive at McNeil Sanctuary, Larry Aumiller sets up camp. Then he makes daily forays from the camping area to observe the bears before the salmon run begins. As a result he has often witnessed the courting and mating antics of the bruins in the vicinity of another, smaller creek where the salmon run begins earlier than that in McNeil River. Among the facts he has learned is that winter hibernation serves as a healing or recuperation period, as well as a long sleep for many of the bruins.

The biologist recalls, for example, a bear that had

survived a furious fight with a stronger male while fishing the river in late July. The last time Aumiller saw that one in August, a large patch of hide had been ripped from its flank, and it walked with a limp. But when first seen again the following May, the bear showed no sign whatever of the injuries.

Another male, known as Patch Butt from a distinctive marking on its rump, had suffered a jaw injury when as a cub it was attacked by a large female. By the age of 16 Patch Butt was still having trouble eating by each season's end. But probably because it did not have to use its jaws and teeth all winter, it always recovered sufficiently to survive another year.

Patch Butt was just one memorable, easy-to-identify bear in the McNeil family album—or rogue's gallery—that Larry Aumiller introduced to Peggy and me. Consider some individuals. Flashman had a long, horse face and seemed to shed his coat later than the others. He always looked ragged. We learned soon to know Chaser by the gold tinge on the shoulders of an otherwise dark brown body; he weighed at least 1,000 pounds. Rex had very long fur on the flanks, and Scarface was not quite as aggressive as his battle-marked visage suggested. When viewed head on, Little Dark Monkey Face was aptly named. From the way he walked, Rusty may have been suffering from arthritis and had fallen somewhat in the McNeil hierarchy. On the way up was RC (for Reggie's Cub), an agile, active youngster growing fast.

White, a 16-year-old female when we photographed her in 1986 and one of triplet cubs (the others were Red and Blue), was so named because she and her siblings had been tranquilized and ear tagged on the Fourth of July. Ladybird, the most dominant and irritable female on the river and about 25 years old, had not had a cub for the past eight years. Normally brown-bear sows have cubs every fourth year throughout their maturity. Goldie was another female easy to distinguish because of long, yellow foreclaws.

From time to time Aumiller has autopsied brown bears on the Alaska Peninsula beyond the McNeil River. Some of his findings may be surprising. All have worms, often very large infestations. Judging from calcium deposits in the joints of many, arthritis is common and must at times be painful. And considering the incredible tooth problems (which must also be painful) in bears of all ages, but especially the older ones, it is remarkable how well they get along when fishing in proximity to one another.

During his early summer investigations, Aumiller has encountered many of the other creatures that share the brown bear's world from water pipits and plovers to red foxes and wolverines. Normally the bruins seemed not to notice any of these. But one day while skirting a low area where beavers had built a system of dams and lodges, the biologist began to notice bear

Two old-timers, probably long-time rivals, now sated with salmon, bask peacefully in the weak Alaskan sun. One is dozing on its feet.

scat and beaver bones. Then just ahead he saw a bear wade out across a pond and climb onto a beaver lodge.

Aumiller recalls that at first the animal sniffed and scratched tentatively, as if mildly curious about the structure. But as Aumiller continued to watch through binoculars, the bear became more and more excited, soon furiously throwing twigs, then even logs, in all directions, tearing the house apart down to water level. After eight or nine minutes of digging, the bear emerged with a yearling beaver, which it immediately ate. Aumiller was surprised at how deliberately, almost daintily, the bear consumed the animal, almost as if prolonging the pleasure of the meal, perhaps because no other bears who might have wanted to share it were in sight.

During recent summers Larry Aumiller has had an assistant manager named Polly Hessing on the river and this permits both more time to make important observations. A tall, energetic, and capable biologist from New Mexico, Hessing leads many of the daily treks from McNeil campsite to the observation bluff above the falls. One of the most rewarding, most exciting photo sessions we've ever known began with Hessing one cool afternoon.

Because ocean tides of 16 to 17 feet are not uncommon along the Alaska Peninsula, there are periods each day at high tide when part of the trail is covered with water too deep to cross even wearing hipboots. We got off to a late start because we waited for the tide to retreat. But once across the flooded area, with only an inch or two of our boot tops dry, we reached a large mud flat. Here the ground was crisscrossed with brown-bear paw prints of all sizes. In several places the bears had been digging for clams. (Earlier Aumiller had told us that some brown bears become busy clam diggers, apparently able to go directly to an underground bivalve and dig it out. The bear then chews the whole clam to bits, shell and all, and swallows it.) Gradually bear tracks funneled onto the single trail and we continued onward, climbing upward toward the falls, our boot prints atop those of the bears. Size 13 boot prints never looked so small.

No matter how many times I make that hike, there is always the uneasy feeling that a bear might be crouched only a few feet away in the waist-deep grass on either side of the path. Once or twice we *have* met bruins *on* the trail, but by pausing for a while, we give them time to move on. I also have *heard* bears moving unseen in the vegetation along the way, but not one has ever been troublesome. The nervous talking and noise of hikers gives bears plenty of warning that the group is coming.

The first sight of the McNeil Falls from a low hill nearby is one impossible ever to forget. On this after-

noon there were only 16 bears in sight, most of them in the water. But Polly pointed to the ridges on both sides of the river where we counted six more. In the afternoon sunlight, which is not a frequent blessing in that maritime region, the wild scene of screaming gulls, a raven, and a bald eagle, all poaching from the bears, was especially memorable.

What we witnessed that eventful afternoon were more than the normal number of confrontations and interactions. The salmon run was just beginning, and the full complement of bears had not yet arrived. We watched as a lot of rank was being established, which would remain unchanged for the entire season. One thing we saw immediately was that on average, the bears on the near side of the river were less dominant, lower ranking, than those on the far side. When Ladybird arrived on the opposite bank to stake out a section of river (where we could clearly see the shadows of many fish) the bears that had given ground crossed the river in our direction. One of twin cubs following its displaced mother was swept away by the current. The cub drifted dangerously close to where several males were fishing, and immediately the mother raced to rescue the frightened, squalling baby. By threatening and rushing at the males, all larger than herself, she managed to retrieve the youngster. Just afterward I noticed that my own pulse had speeded up again.

We had a good opportunity that afternoon to compare and to photograph the different fishing techniques of the bears. From the time of arrival until they stalk away with bulging stomachs, some bears are simply more expert fishers than others. Polly Hessing strongly suspects that fishing techniques are either inherited or learned from the example of the mother. We watched one sow with cubs easily catch a fish every time she waded into the water, while another of similar age and size had a more difficult time. Of course good location has a lot to do with success, but it is far from being the only factor.

Some of the top-ranking bears could just stand motionless in a shallow funnel where salmon paused before trying to leap the falls. These bears could easily seize with their teeth any fish swimming between their forefeet. Another successful technique is to trap salmon in shallow eddies and then pounce on them. Many bears exert a lot more energy than finesse when they seem to lunge at any passing shadow, and still others try to catch salmon by swimming underwater. This doesn't work very well. One bear we photographed perched on a ledge and lurched headlong into

We met this bear suddenly on the trail to McNeil Falls. After studying us for a moment, it vanished in the waist-deep grass.

the water at each passing school, a fishing method doomed to failure.

A few of the more agile and aggressive bears do not bother to get wet at all. They get enough to eat by playing the waiting game and robbing better fishermen of their catch when it's brought ashore. This can cause a ripple of dissent throughout the bear community along the river. But at least one of the bears, a quick and nervous female who was also an expert angler, did not seem to resent giving up half the fish she caught in return for tranquility in her sector.

Most females with smaller cubs keep them well back from water's edge, usually huddled together, while fishing for the family. Most cubs remain where they are put, but a few impatient or precocious ones go into the water to "help" with the fishing. More often than not when a sow returns to shore with one salmon for two or three cubs, brotherly love is instantly forgotten in a sharp contest to decide which gets most or all of the fish. The fighting among cubs for food, unrestrained by the mother, may be as bitter as any battles for rank among the large males.

Late in the afternoon I was intently focused on the great dark male, Rusty, feeding on a fresh salmon not 40 feet from my tripod. My long telephoto lens brought me near enough to see the salmon eggs dribbling out of the bruin's bloody mouth. That's when Polly Hessing pointed to something entirely different and farther away. A female red breasted merganser with a brood of 12 ducklings was drifting down the center of the river in the strongest current, directly toward the falls and the bears.

Almost at the brink, the hen turned back but only six of the ducklings managed to follow her. The rest were swept over and down "death canyon" toward two dozen hungry bears. Glaucous-winged gulls, always on hand to clean up bear scraps, immediately pounced on three ducklings. Once in calmer water, the three survivors swam directly to shore, actually frightening one bear in the process. Another bear picked up a chick, seemed to mouth it for a moment and dropped it. Miraculously, to me, all three ducklings made it to the bank and through the bear gauntlet to rejoin their diminished family above the falls.

Earlier I mentioned one young bear, RC, which was growing rapidly and promised to be one of the dominant McNeil males of the future. This day at the falls we saw why. After arriving on the river, RC established what may be very close to a record for gluttony by catching and eating 14 chum salmon, 7 to

Rusty, an old male bear, spent much time feeding, sleeping, and studying us as we photographed him from the McNeil photo platform.

12 pounds apiece, without pausing. During one period the animal was recycling a fish every six minutes.

While RC was halfway through his dinner, we saw another bear catch a salmon right at the top of the falls. At the same time it was attacked by another bear whose fishing territory it had invaded. The first toppled backward over the falls and was caught in a chute of white water that carried it far downstream past other, surprised fishing bears. After finally regaining its footing in shallow water and *still* clutching its prize, the bear raced for dense willow cover on the shore and disappeared. There are very few dull moments on the McNeil River.

At twilight we packed camera gear into backpacks and began the bittersweet trek back to camp; bitter because I was tired and my shoulders ached, sweet because of the incomparable spectacle we had watched all afternoon. But there was more. On reaching the McNeil Lagoon, glittering silver in the twilight, we saw a sow leading three offspring, born the past winter, toward water to cross ahead of us. Two of the cubs readily followed the mother, swimming just behind her. But the third, which seemed smaller than the others, balked and bawled pitifully until the female returned and half coaxed, half forced the reluctant cub into the water. The last we saw of them, all emerged dripping and shaking on the opposite shore. Again the smallest one had fallen far behind, and we wondered if it would survive the summer.

By radio we had made plans to leave McNeil the next afternoon when a Kachemak Air floatplane could land nearby at high tide. But because of weather and other unforeseen problems, schedules are not always kept in wilderness Alaska. Delays are commonplace, and our plane would not be able to pick us up until *after* the high tide period and then not unless we could somehow signal one of the commercial salmon boats anchored near McNeil camp to ferry us out into open Shelikof Strait where our plane would be. Thus, for the first time in our lives, we boarded an aircraft actually at sea, jumping from the boat to a pontoon tip on the heaving swells of the ocean. I would not want to do that every day.

We were relieved to be airborne in the rose-gray light of evening. As usual Augustine Island was smoking, a thin plume rising from the peak. Soon we could see the lights of Homer on the Kenai Peninsula. We landed in near darkness and were soon asleep at the Homer public campground.

At low tide, a mother bear leads three cubs across the tidal flats of McNeil Lagoon. Notice how much smaller the first cub is than the other two. As we watched from a distance, it soon fell behind. We wondered if it would survive.

CHAPTER NINE

An Island Called Afognak

August 26, 1979, a day I will not forget. Shortly after daybreak I smell the rich aroma of coffee in my darkened room. Through a cabin window I can see the first shafts of lemon light penetrating the dense forest of Sitka spruce. Then comes a rap on our door, and a voice says, "Six-thirty." A few minutes later Peggy and I are dressed, although still a little groggy.

Downstairs the kitchen is fragrant and busy. The coffee clears the corners of our brains. While Shannon Randall stirs a bowl of sourdough pancake batter laced with wild elderberries, fingers of battered halibut are deep-frying to gold on a huge stove. Roy Randall stares through the kitchen window, across the smooth surface of Seal Bay toward the Gulf of Alaska, which also is calm beneath a haze low over the water.

"The barometer is holding high," he says, "and the wind is down. My guess is we'll have another fair day."

The four of us sit down to a meal big enough for twice as many. Peggy comments that this just may be the biggest, most delicious breakfast she has ever had. I can't disagree. Roy only smiles. It's routine for him.

The meal finished, we all four climb down a steep catwalk to the Randall's floating dock where two boats are tied. The tide is low, leaving a vast expanse of undersea life exposed along the rocky shoreline. We carry armloads of fishing tackle and cameras. The outboard coughs and complains before starting, but soon we are planing out across the open water.

Close to shore and around eroded offshore islands, Roy must carefully weave his way through fields of giant kelp. We watch several blacktail deer silhouetted against the sunrise on a large island. The world's greatest concentration of sea otters surrounds Afognak

SELECTED SITES FROM THIS CHAPTER

Island, and we count almost 100 of them lazing on the surface until the boat skims too close. Then they dive, but quickly resurface in our wake. A few allow us to come very near before disappearing.

Once we are riding the swells out on the open gulf, Roy aims his boat directly south. Although it is not really a cold morning, Peggy and I are accustomed to the low humidity of Wyoming, so we shiver deep inside our down-filled parkas until the sun is well above the horizon and the gray haze evaporates. We enjoy smooth running until we reach the ocean current that surges through Marmot Strait. There we bounce through a rough chop. An hour later the boat ap-

Steller's sea lions haul out on the rocky islets of Cape Tonki, windswept and wild. Here we also usually found brown bears prowling the beaches.

161

Sea otters are as easy to see on Afognak as anywhere. But it is quite unusual to spot them on land, as we did here.

proaches Marmot Island, and abruptly the sea is smooth again. Long before we can see them, we hear the din of more than 12,000 Steller's sea lions that live on this distant, uninhabited chunk of Alaska.

Along the clifflike east shore of Marmot Island, as far as we can see, the upthrust rocks, gravel beaches, and surf are swarming, alive with sea lions. There are scattered herds of bachelor bulls, but most animals are sleek cows, with masses of coal-black, shiny pups. A few spotted harbor seals are among them. Some of the animals only watch us and bellow, but many, many more—masses of them—swim out to follow us, barking all the while.

We are surrounded by the sea lions. Here and there the sea seethes with them. At times we are close enough to smell the strong fishy stench that lingers over every beach in the world where marine mammals haul out. Even in a career devoted largely to wildlife and wildlife photography, I realize this visit to Marmot Island is extraordinary. It matches anything we have ever found on the dusty plains of Africa or in any other remote corner of the world. We expose many rolls of film.

When the wind freshens, Roy is forced to turn back toward Afognak Island, which is indented almost all around with sheltered bays and coves. He retreats in to one of these. We wade ashore onto a pebble beach and a scene almost as remarkable as the sea-lion haul-out on Marmot Island.

Here an alcohol-clear stream, perhaps 50 feet wide, races over shallow riffles to reach salt water. Schooled up—no, crushed and crammed—into the mouth of the stream are sockeye salmon. Most are still bright and silvery, but among them are individuals turning pink with spawning color. A few are bright scarlet. We watch the salmon for a few moments, but since we'd missed lunch, we select a rock overlooking the sockeye stream and sit in the sunshine munching sandwiches and chocolate bars.

Suddenly Shannon notices that we are not the only fish watchers present. A small brown bear has emerged from the red-berried devil's club shrub below us and waded well out into the current, scattering salmon. It sees us, then stands briefly, woofs softly, and quickly disappears. I am a little nervous as I proceed to catch our evening dinner in that same spot a little later. This small brown bear weighed about 300 pounds.

A long, cool Alaskan twilight has begun as we return to the Randalls' Afognak Wilderness Lodge, snug inside, with a fire glowing in a stone fireplace. The Randalls' daughter, Inga, has coffee brewing and venison chops ready to be broiled, along with the salmon. A perfect end of an extraordinary day! As we sip the coffee, Roy recalls days that were not so perfect.

EARLY DAYS AND AFOGNAK LODGE. On a cold, blustery afternoon in 1964, Roy and his hunting partner, Harold Lane, were cruising slowly through Marmot Strait, the turbulent passage that divides Afognak and Kodiak islands, when they saw several seals on the shore. Roy disembarked to begin a stalk while Harold retreated to wait aboard the boat out in open water. It was then that the world began to shudder violently. This was the beginning of the worst earthquake ever recorded in Alaska.

"The first shock knocked me off my feet," Roy remembers, "and I had to lie flat through tremor after tremor to keep from being bounced around. Sometime just afterward, a massive tidal wave crashed onto shore, then all of the water was sucked out of a small bay. I can still see vividly the brilliantly colored bottom life suddenly exposed to air, before water surged back into the bay again. It was unreal and terrible. I figured it was the end. Somehow Harold kept his cool, crept close enough to pick me up, and we floundered for the safety of open water.

"Maybe most of all I'll never forget what we heard on our boat radio. Frantic calls for help were crackling back and forth. We heard a fishing vessel skipper we knew shout, 'Here it comes, (a wave) 100 feet tall and straight at us. If we make this one, boys, I'll see you all at home.' He didn't make it. Nor did lots of others. In fact the not-too-distant town of Kodiak was practically destroyed. Somehow we rode it out.

"But once the earthquake passed, and I could stand squarely on solid ground again, I wondered what I was doing in Alaska. Fortunately I didn't wonder too long."

Roy Randall came to Alaska in 1961 at the age of 28. He had been drifting from Kentucky to college in Texas to California in more jobs than he can now recall, always a serious outdoorsman and a "gun nut." Sometime along the way he read an item in *Outdoor Life* magazine about seal hunting and homesteading in what was then the territory of Alaska. The article was so glowing, so compelling, that he packed up his rifles and what little else he owned and headed north, bumming and stone broke.

In those days, a tough and determined person actually could make a living seal hunting. Harbor seals were abundant along Alaskan coasts. The hides were used to manufacture coats, parkas, boots, and other garments, and there has always been at least a modest market for them. Sometimes seals would plunder

Roy Randall relaxing and wife Shannon, here demonstrating how she peeled the logs for their Afognak Wilderness Lodge.

A view of the boat dock from the Randalls'
Afognak Wilderness Lodge. This place is a haven
for fishermen, naturalists, and photographers.
Right: A spotted harbor seal takes a stretcher.

salmon nets. Commercial fishermen so despised them
that in 1927 a bounty was placed on the animals, so
seals could be shot for the bounty as well as for their
hide.

Until 1967 when the bounty was eliminated, more
than $1 million was paid to hunters. But too great a
demand for the skins, diminishing seal numbers, and
skyrocketing prices not only ended the bounty, but
resulted in closed seasons and bag limits. Some of the
hunting pressure was shifted onto Alaska's sea lions,
which remained abundant.

Seal hunting in Alaska was a hard, perilous way to
make a living. A hunter had to thrive on cold, rough
seas. Always threatening was the danger of slipping
or falling into icy water. Roy did fall in once, over
his head, but somehow won a race with death to a
warm camp where he shivered for days and again con-
templated his future. Of course he continued to hunt
and became one of the most efficient of all, operating
from a rugged cabin, barely 12 × 12 feet, which he
built himself beside Seal Bay, a sheltered cove of Afognak. He selected that site because of the shelter it
offered in any weather and because "it was the love-
liest place" he had ever seen. Only four other people
lived on the 40 × 25-mile island, none of them nearby. Randall admits to becoming almost a recluse.

One fall day while buying supplies in Kodiak, Roy
had dinner with a friend whose niece happened to be
visiting from Toronto. A comely legal secretary, the
niece regarded Roy with curiosity.

"What's your work?" she asked.

"Sealing," he answered defensively. "Anything
wrong with that?"

"No, not really. I'd like to try it."

A few days later she did.

From that moment until the Marine Mammals Act
of 1972 ended seal hunting, Shannon and Roy Randall

164

were inseparable hunting partners. It was exciting, exhilarating, high adventure.

They made an efficient hunting team. A team normally requires a "shooter" and a "skiff man." Shannon was the skiff man. The two cruised distant shorelines and forgotten islands, straining through fog and sleet to find hauled-out seals, after which Roy was put ashore out of sight, often on the opposite side of an island. He would then stalk, infantry-style, to a point from which he could shoot as many seals as possible. Each shot had to count; each bullet had to hit the brain to anchor the target right in place. If a wounded seal ever reached the water it was lost. When Roy began hunting seals, he used a .243 with 75-grain

bullets; later he used a .22 Hornet with 46-grain loads. He once made 54 one-shot, on-the-spot kills in succession.

When the Marine Mammals Act of 1972 outlawed sealing, Roy and Shannon Randall were suddenly out of business. Their daughter, Inga, was still a baby, and a second child was on the way when they had to make the all-important decision: stay or go.

"We made our choice one bitter evening," Roy recalls. "Our cabin on Seal Bay was home; we couldn't leave it. Maybe it was crazy, but instead of quitting, we decided to build a bigger, more comfortable place which would be a wilderness lodge for a few guests as well as our own dwelling. It seemed to me that others would also enjoy this paradise. I figured I would make a good guide."

Lacking tools and funds, as well as construction experience, they built by hand, from the foundation up, a 12-room structure that blends neatly into its lush forest environment. More than 300 logs, all cut some distance away and towed by boat to the site, formed the main part of the building, which Shannon had designed and sketched on scrap paper. She peeled all of those logs by hand and worked like a stevedore. The couple could afford no heavy equipment, not even a chain saw. They combed some materials from nearby beaches and scrounged the windows from abandoned military barracks in Kodiak, 50 miles away by sea. From start to finish there were virtually no cash outlays for anything except nails.

One evening a bear broke into their old cabin and guzzled $500 worth of seal oil that they had collected during legal sealing and had cached as a contingency fund. Roy had to shoot that bear one night when it tried to climb into the bedroom, presumably in search of more oil.

Late in 1974 the Randalls settled into their new lodge. Since then two guest cabins have been built near the lodge. For the past few years, serious outdoors enthusiasts from all over the United States and Europe have come to spend a week or so with the Randalls. For most it is the trip of their lives. Some come in spring to hunt Alaska brown bears, which reach their maximum size on Afognak and Kodiak. From late summer through fall, many of the visitors are deer or elk hunters.

But most guests by far arrive during golden summertime to enjoy the excellent fishing and the wild-

life, or simply to escape to an Alaska still primeval and unpolluted. Red, or sockeye, salmon run from mid-June to mid-July. Pinks, or humpback, salmon come next, spawning until August. Silvers, or cohos, are abundant around the mouths of Afognak rivers, until mid-September. The silver-salmon fishing borders on the sensational.

AFOGNAK'S BLACKTAILS AND SILVERS.
Despite its remoteness, the Randalls' lodge is only a day away from almost anywhere in North America, thanks to daily jets from Seattle to Kodiak. From Kodiak it is only a 20-minute charter flight by floatplane to Seal Bay. One afternoon toward the end of August 1979, an arriving flight carried Horst and Erica Rothmeier of West Germany and Milt and Mary Moss of Anchorage. The Rothmeiers were after the silver salmon then reaching the peak of their runs into Afognak streams. The Mosses wanted to hunt blacktails as well as the silvers. Peggy and I joined them.

Sitka blacktail deer are native to southeastern Alaskan forests, but not to Afognak. Along with Roosevelt elk, the small deer were stocked on the island about 40 years ago by the old U.S. Biological Survey. Apparently the new home agreed with both because today they are numerous. The limits are five or six a person. But hunting the animal is not easy. Nor is it very similar to deer hunting elsewhere— hunting here is done from a boat.

Well before sunrise we pushed off from the Randall dock and, in the mist and eerie morning light, began a systematic search of the headlands, the peninsulas and large islands that are separated from Afognak by the 20-foot high tides. For an hour or two after daybreak the deer stroll out onto grassy edges to feed.

We saw the deer almost wherever there were forest openings or green meadows adjacent to the sea. Nine does and fawns fed in one herd, four in another, then five, and soon we lost track of the total. Then rounding a point of land where a steep wooded island had been temporarily cut off from mainland Afognak by the tide, Roy cut the throttle and pointed to a high bluff. There against the first rosy glow of the rising sun stood two deer. Even at long range we could see that both had antlers.

"Forkhorn bucks," Roy said after studying them through his binoculars, "and in a good place to make a drive."

The strategy was to put Milt Moss ashore where the tidal channel split the small island from Afognak. Then after anchoring the boat on the island's opposite side, Roy, Peggy, and I would make a quick drive toward the hunter. In contrast to too many other deer drives I could recall in years past, this one worked.

Neither Roosevelt elk (top) nor Sitka blacktail deer are native to Afognak. Both are thriving today after introduction by the U. S. Biological Survey in the 1940s.

One buck broke immediately toward the nearest pebble beach, where (with a telephoto lens) I shot it plunging into the salt water to swim to safety. The other bounded directly toward Milt, who easily collected it. By the time we field-dressed and loaded the blacktail into the boat, the sun was well above the horizon.

What followed should happen to every serious fisherman some day. It was a half-hour's run to where a small, meandering river, unnamed on any map, emptied into a secluded cove. A boater might easily cruise past it time and again without ever knowing the river existed. Near its mouth it is almost completely canopied by evergreens. But by following an ages-old bear trail for several hundred yards along the bank, we came upon a series of clear, pools bordered by emerald velvet moss. The last pool upstream was fed by a 10-foot waterfall. The pools were full of both silver and sockeye salmon, fresh and bright from the ocean, pausing before beginning the final run up and over the falls to spawning sites.

I do not remember who made the first cast. But I will never forget the first silver that tasted a metal spinner. It raced toward the falls and, in the single shaft of sunshine that penetreated the forest gloom, leaped a good 3 feet clear of the water. Spray flew as sparks of light. Line peeled from someone's reel. The salmon jumped a second time and was free. Another fish struck the second cast and it too catapulted to freedom.

We stayed only long enough to catch a salmon or two apiece, which we immediately released. Fishing was simply too easy. Fresh trails, paw prints, and partially eaten fish all around told us that that exquisite place belonged to bruins. Big ones at that.

"Besides," Roy promised, "there are several other streams not far from here where more and bigger salmon are running. Some of the silvers go to 12 pounds and more."

He wasn't exaggerating. During the next few days we angled for salmon in what may be the fastest sport in the state. But we didn't have the fishing entirely to ourselves. As you might guess, the other fishermen we met were brown bears.

BEARS AND OTHER WILDLIFE. August 29, 1979. As always, Roy is circulating before daybreak,

and after putting a pot of coffee to brew on the stove, he comes rapping on our door. Peggy and I dress and hurry down a spiral log staircase to a warm kitchen where Shannon is mixing an omelet.

"I have to pull the halibut stake and a couple of prawn traps," Roy says, "and I could use a little extra muscle power. Also the humpbacks are choking a stream about an hour from here. If we get there early

By small boat on a calm sea, it is a two-hour run from Afognak Lodge to Marmot Island and probably the world's largest Steller's sea lion rookery. We approached shore to photograph a few of the 12,000 animals there.

enough we can probably find a couple of bears fishing for them."

"Count us in," I answer.

As always the early morning on the Gulf of Alaska is cold and damp, but the run to the halibut stake, which is really a multihook trotline anchored in a bay about 20 fathoms deep, is short. We drift close to a rose-colored plastic buoy, pull it into the boat, and then begin the tough, hand-over-hand task of pulling up the stake. We haven't pulled very far before we know something alive is on the line.

"If it's a halibut small enough to handle," Roy began his instructions, "you take it with the gaff. If it's too big, I'll have to plug it with the pistol. Two weeks ago we had one just under 200 pounds. I had to shoot it to boat it."

This time, however, there is just one fish on the line, about 30 pounds. I gaff it and swing it, still fighting, into the boat. It hammers on the bottom. We rebait all the empty hooks with the heads and tails of salmon and lower the stake back into the water. Not far away we raise a couple of prawn traps from deep water, also by arm power alone, and harvest a large bucket of colorful spotted shrimp.

"No matter what happens the rest of this day," Peggy comments, "it can't be better than dinner will be tonight."

Virtually all our dinners at Afognak are products of what we've caught or picked or collected ourselves. Besides a variety of seafood, that bounty includes wild berries, angel wing and hedgehog mushrooms, and the kelp that grows just beyond the boat dock and makes wonderful pickles.

After leaving the morning's seafood harvest at the lodge, Roy aims his boat northward and then westward around the irregular Afognak coast, all the while within sight and sound of astronomical numbers of seabirds. As we pass one small island, 100 sea lions see us, and some of them splash headlong into the surf. Rounding a thin, shallow point, Roy swings sharply left. We enter a long and narrow cove, eventually anchoring beside the mouth of what at first appears to be a sluggish river. Wearing the thigh-high rubber boots that are indispensable hereabouts, we wade ashore.

"Bear trails parallel both sides of this river," Roy explains. "We'll walk up one side—carefully—watching ahead and also watching for telltale signs from birds. There ought to be a bear within the next half mile. Several are practically living here."

The camera in my hand doesn't seem like much protection, especially considering the huge paw prints sunk deep in soft earth. They are bigger than even my own size 13 boots. Peggy gulps. But Roy, who leads the way, carries a .30/06, so I feel better. We haven't gone very far when suddenly, around a bend, we startle a bald eagle. Beating its broad wings, it has trouble getting airborne after gorging on salmon.

I have never seen a waterway as full of fish as this. Almost every square foot seems alive, boiling with pink salmon. We walk slowly and marvel. I forget for a minute about the bears. Then Roy stops. He has seen several gulls flare, squalling, from a hidden pool ahead. Something flushed them.

"Our bear should be right there," he says softly.

Slowly we move ahead, up onto a low knoll. From

A red-throated loon sits motionless on a nest while I focus a telephoto lens. This species spends the entire year around Afognak and Kodiak islands.

that viewpoint the bruin is clearly visible, about 75 yards away. We watch it splash into the center of the stream, lunge at one fish, miss it, and then catch another, which it drags, flopping into tall grass out of sight.

"We can move a little closer," Roy suggests.

When the bear returns to the water it is only 35 or 40 yards away. Through my 400mm telephoto lens I can see salmon blood on its muzzle. Suddenly the bear stands erect, dripping, and stares directly toward

us. It is bigger than average, brown, probably male. I wonder how it could possibly have heard my camera's motor drive above the steady rush of the stream and splash of the salmon. But in a moment it drops again to all fours and catches three or four more salmon. After the last salmon, we do not see the big brute again.

September 1, 1979. It is bright and sunny, which is a welcome bonus in a part of the world where weather tends toward gray and gloomy. We spend most of the day fishing for silver and humpback salmon near the mouth of a scenic river with Roy and the German guests, Horst and Erica Rothmeier. Horst, who has sampled some of the blue-ribbon salmon waters of Europe, cannot believe what is happening to him here. By noon he has taken 10 salmon: 5 beautiful leaping silvers and 5 humpies. He now knows, he says smiling, how those early prospectors felt when they found gold in the Klondike and on Nome's beaches.

Peggy and I also catch a couple of cohos on spinning tackle, and since it seems so easy that way, I rig up a fly rod and knot a red-and-white marabou streamer onto my leader. I wade out knee-deep to cast, where fresh water meets tide water. Salmon are breaking water all over. Quickly I retrieve the fly and when I'm just about ready to pick it up for another cast, a fish strikes and in the same split second heads toward Hawaii, jumping all the way. I raise the rod tip too sharply and reel in a snapped leader. Pound for pound, those silver salmon must rank with the best gamefish in the world.

After losing another streamer fly, I finally do hook a silver, then 15 minutes later, another. It is a time anyone who relishes fishing in a remote paradise would always remember.

AFOGNAK'S FUTURE. Perhaps it is a poor idea to end an otherwise happy and exciting adventure story on a sour note. If you agree, stop reading here. But something more must be added because Afognak Island is a national treasure and there are plans afoot to reduce it to something much less. Some call it progress; I call it pillage.

Much of Afognak is covered with mature Sitka spruce, which is today considered harvestable. Until recently the forest resources on the island, part of the Chugach National Forest, were managed by the U.S. Forest Service. But management now belongs to Alaskan natives as part of the native settlement claims, and that is pure disaster. Timbering rights have been sold to a Japanese firm. Right now the forests of Afognak are being cut—clear-cut—in a manner that has already destroyed too many other precious woodlands in America for a fast buck. A heavy truck road has sliced almost completely across the island so that trees can be moved out faster.

"Does anyone know that it takes a Sitka spruce 75 years to grow to a 10-inch diameter?" Roy asks.

In view of the current forestry practices now underway in so much of Alaska's timber areas (the lumber is actually sold for less than it costs to harvest it) plus the dangers to Afognak Island, we need to take a new look at what is happening in America today. All outdoors people and conservationists, in fact all of us, have a heavy stake in it. With enough protests from concerned citizens to their senators and congressmen, these woodlands can be managed in a responsible, rather than a destructive, way and pristine areas like Afognak Island preserved.

A bear found a sea lion carcass we used as bait and began to feed on it. But when bad weather prevented our returning for several days, we found very little bait remaining.

172

There's gold and it's haunting and haunting;
It's luring me on as of old;
Yet it isn't the gold that I'm wanting
So much as just finding the gold.
It's the great, big, broad land way up yonder,
It's the forests where silence has lease;
It's the beauty that thrills me with wonder;
It's the stillness that fills me with peace.

—Robert Service

CHAPTER TEN

Gold of the Yukon

Although this Canadian Territory, which shares a 750-mile border with Alaska, has changed somewhat since poet Robert Service saw it early in the 20th century, much remains a pristine land of extraordinary beauty and adventure, of stillness and peace. The nuggets and mother lodes that gold rush stampeders sought in the Klondike and beyond early in this century are not—never were—the true treasure of the Yukon. Instead it's the wilderness and wildlife. Peggy and I devoted a recent spring to prospecting for this true gold.

HEADING FOR THE YUKON. The roundabout way we reached the Yukon and our main destination, the Dempster Highway, is worth describing in some detail. Until the Dalton Highway, perhaps better known as the "north slope haul road," is fully opened to public travel, the Dempster will wind farther north than any other road on the continent. The Dalton parallels the Alaska Oil Pipeline 416 miles from Livengood, Alaska, north to Prudhoe Bay. Beginning near the gold rush camp at Dawson on Yukon's Klondike Highway, the Dempster probes all the way north past Fort McPherson and Arctic Red River, there crossing the wide Mackenzie river, to a terminus at Inuvik just short of the Beaufort Sea. We did not plan to explore that far, in fact no farther than the Ogilvie Mountains where our research revealed that wildlife was most abundant. That wilderness range was still deeply snow-covered and its rivers frozen fast when we left home in Wyoming on May 3d. Blame our eagerness to get going on the long, hard winter we had just endured in the Tetons.

From Wyoming we drove our VW van, stocked with everything a pair of photographers would need, directly to Port Angeles, Washington. There we caught the British Columbia ferry to Victoria on

Vancouver Island and continued north via Port Alberni to camp for a few days in Pacific Rim National Park. Like most other units of Parks Canada, Pacific Rim is a beautiful natural area. A thin strip of Pacific rain forest bordering the ocean forms a sort of oasis from the almost total destruction that has occurred elsewhere to the forests of Vancouver Island (as well as to much of mainland British Columbia). A year after making that drive northward over the entire length of Vancouver Island, Victoria to Port Hardy, Peggy and I visited many areas of Brazil's Amazonia where the rain forests also are being systematically pillaged. But the destruction we saw in Brazil is not nearly as complete or as sickening to see as the senseless clear-cutting that has been permitted during the past decade or two in British Columbia. There simply is no excuse for these criminal forest practices that bring quick, short-term economic gain. We deplore this kind of thing when it takes place in the Third World, but seem silent when it occurs closer to home.

As if the drive on Vancouver Island was not unpleasant enough, we reached Port Hardy to learn that a tsunami watch was in effect. An earthquake in the Aleutian Islands was expected to send a tidal wave rolling toward southeast Alaska and the British Columbia coast, so we spent the night "camped" in the parking lot of a Safeway supermarket high above the harbor. However the tsunami did not show up. The next morning we caught a connecting car ferry via Bella Bella for Prince Rupert. From the boat deck we could see that the vicious clear-cutting of British Columbia forests was not limited to Vancouver Island. Bare stumps stood forlornly on mile after mile of steep, eroding hillsides.

May 10th. We finally board the Alaska Marine Highway, the auto ferry M/V *Taku*, which is only about half filled at this time of year, and continue northward. We arrive in Ketchikan on a rare sunny day there. But it is raining as we dock later at Juneau and pass the entrance to Glacier Bay. We debark in Skagway midafternoon on May 11th, and from there drive on the fine, newly paved road toward Yukon's

Golden eagles nest in craggy places along the Dempster Highway, and here Peggy photographed a young bird that had just captured a willow ptarmigan and was unwilling to leave it.

175

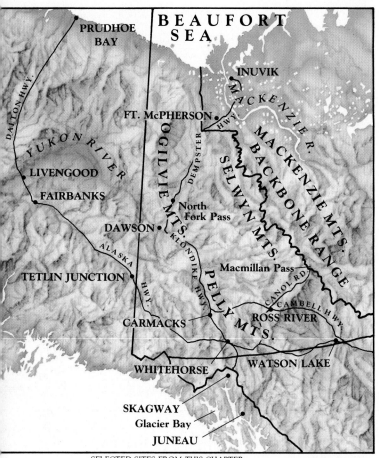

SELECTED SITES FROM THIS CHAPTER

DEMPSTER HIGHWAY WILDLIFE. May 14th. Early in the morning we leave the Klondike Highway, the last supply point for gasoline and groceries, and after filling our fuel cans, turn northward on the Dempster. The highway was named after a Northwest Mounted Police corporal who in 1911 recovered the bodies of four fellow constables lost on a winter arctic patrol.

Barely out of sight of the Klondike road junction, a sharptailed grouse glided low across the right-of-way and landed in a clearing just to our left. I hit the brake and came to a stop almost beside a lek, or strutting ground. In the center of the clearing two cocks were circling one another while several hens around them nibbled on low vegetation.

Caught totally unprepared, we fumbled for some minutes for cameras and tripods in our cargo. Meanwhile the male sharptails faced one another with lavender neck sacs inflated and heads down, then time and again turned to show their profiles. But our sudden stop had made them nervous. By the time we were ready to photograph, all had moved farther away. Still this was a fascinating ritual to watch—the first time we had ever found a sharptail grouse lek, and despite the too-distant subjects, the encounter was a great beginning for our Dempster adventure.

Travel would be slow. Though lower elevations were snow-free, snow patches remained higher up. The road's crown was rough and often had a washboard surface, while the edges were soft, the result of spring thaw. We could keep to the center of the road because during our first day we did not meet another vehicle. Slushy snow still covered North Fork and Windy passes in the Ogilvies. Probably our unfamiliarity with the road, plus the wet snow that began to fall on Windy Pass, prevented us from seeing much wildlife. We did spot one fine Dall ram with full-curl horns, standing alone on a steep, dark slope above us. As we studied him through field glasses, he disappeared into the swirling snow. We covered only 120 miles all day, overnighting in the van in one of the few places where it was possible to drive a short distance off the road.

Next morning, May 15th, we awoke to a vastly different, brighter world. The early sun quickly melted the four inches of snow that had accumulated on the van. We ate breakfast while the world outside our windows came alive. A male willow ptarmigan in half-white, half-brown plumage perched and cackled on top of a stunted evergreen nearby. A pair of golden plovers flew to the ground close by and began to for-

capital, Whitehorse. The road is smooth and perfectly passable, but only because White Pass has just recently been plowed, opening the way through deep drifts. Now, especially, we realize that we are pushing the season this far north. We camp overnight at Takhini Hot Springs north of Whitehorse, wallowing for a long time in the thermal pool.

Before pushing on we also check with old friends Sam Miller, Nan Eagleson, and Norman Barichello in the Whitehorse area. Sam has not yet left to open his wilderness lodge, Oldsquaw, in the Selwyn Mountains on the Yukon–Northwest Territories border (about which I write later in this book). Snow still blocks the Canol Road which he must take. Norman is a Yukon government biologist who has studied birds of prey, gyrfalcons especially, in the Ogilvie Mountains where we are headed. He gives us notebooks full of information about everything from scattered campsites on the Dempster Highway to eagle aeries, waterfowl nesting areas, and where to watch out for grizzly bears. Early traffic, he warned, is virtually nonexistent along the road, and no accommodations or services whatever exist from Dawson northward for almost 200 miles. So we had to borrow several gas cans from him to extend our car travels.

Fireweed grows along the Dempster Highway, here with the Ogilvie Mountains in the background.

An arctic ground squirrel, locally called siksik, is alert beside a moose skull at
Oldsquaw Lodge. The squirrel also gnawed on the antlers. Previous page: In
springtime, willow ptarmigan are easy to see and photograph along Yukon roads.
Then the cocks are establishing breeding territories.

age. A golden crowned sparrow sat for a moment on the rearview mirror outside and regarded us as we drank coffee inside.

It is often amazing what a difference a day makes. Maybe we had been concentrating on driving and the road too much; maybe the brief storm had brought new bird arrivals into the Ogilvie Mountains. For whatever reason, later in the day when we slowly re-traced our route for about 50 miles to return to our campsite, wild creatures were everywhere on the landscape.

Especially ptarmigan. At intervals in the valleys and along stream courses, male willow ptarmigan were either perched above or patrolling their territories, for this was the courtship and mating season. By looking closely we could often see a female or two, much less conspicuous, in the brush. Where the road climbed to higher elevations the courting cocks we saw and photographed were rock rather than willow ptarmigan. We could approach many of the willows to very close camera range.

Pairs of mew gulls were protecting nesting territories along the road, after migration flights from points far

south. We watched the first arctic ground squirrels to emerge from hibernation welcome the warm spring day. Back at Windy Pass where we'd seen the Dall ram in snow swirls the day before, we now counted 14 white ewes, but the male was nowhere in sight.

On every pond or pothole of any size, ducks courted or tipped up to feed around shallow edges. Pintails were the most common species we encountered, with green-winged teal coming next. Some of these birds would remain here to nest; others would continue the trip farther north. One duck we saw, a widgeon drake, would do neither; it had been caught hopping from one pond to another by a northern harrier, which itself would soon nest on the ground nearby.

During the next few days, the roster of wildlife species seemed to increase and change with the lengthening, warming days. Some days we would drive slowly along the road looking for subjects. On others we struck out on foot with backpacks. One almost balmy afternoon, wearing dark sunglasses against the glare, we hiked along the churning Blackstone River, watching chunks of ice break off the banks, grind against gravel, and then clog and form jams at the

179

next downstream bend. Common goldeneye ducks swam among the floes and seemed to be feeding on invisible aquatic creatures. As we watched, we saw a blur of bright orange on the far bank. A red fox was sneaking, sometimes running, sometimes crawling on a path parallel to one goldeneye, intent on catching it. When almost directly opposite, the fox spotted us and gave up its stalk. We regretted halting his hunting, but the sight of the fox in full, long winter fur and hurrying over the snow was beautiful.

Another day on the Blackstone River we had a sudden encounter of a different sort. A strong wind was blowing in our faces as we walked upstream, and that explained why the dark brown grizzly bear, coming downstream, did not catch our scent until we saw each other only about 60 feet apart (later I paced it off). Before I fully appreciated our predicament, the animal turned and was splashing, fighting its way against a powerful current to reach the far river bank. The next sounds I heard were louder than the ice grinding against gravel. They were of my own pulse pounding above it all.

One night, another grizzly passed silently and unseen past our parked van. Paw prints deep in snow and soft earth were the evidence. Judging from the straight path it followed, the animal was not curious enough to pause and inspect us. During that week of driving the Dempster within about 150 miles of the Klondike Highway, we counted six different grizzly bears. One of the encounters was especially exciting.

We had spent most of the morning photographing the only beaver we saw on the trip, on a small pond impounded by an old beaver dam. The pond was still partly covered with a crust of ice, thinning in a few places. At intervals the lone beaver would look up through an ice hole, as if for danger, then disappear to emerge again with a long stringer of green moss or algae, which it ate in full view of our telephoto lenses. We noted that fresh tracks of a grizzly skirted one side of the pond.

When the beaver was finished feeding and had left, we continued down the road by car and, immediately after rounding the first sharp bend, noticed two dark figures in a snow bank about 150 yards ahead. I stopped and cut the motor. Through binoculars these proved to be two medium-size grizzlies engaged in a vigorous, but not angry, wrestling match. One was much darker than the other. Considering the spring season, we judged this to be a mating pair—a rare activity to see at fairly close range.

I saw my first wild wolf on my first trip on the Alaska Highway long ago. Since then we have seen a few others while driving very early or late in the day.

So should we be content to watch at a distance of 150 yards or, with a light crosswind blowing, should we try to move carefully closer into long photographic range? We decided to move closer.

That proved to be a mistake. The instant I touched the starter the two bears abruptly stopped sparring, and looked in our direction. One began to walk away, soon increasing its speed to a lope, and the other followed. Until out of sight at least a half mile away, neither bear looked back at us. I am convinced that grizzlies have far better hearing and vision than is often assumed.

During the next days, increasing numbers of shorebirds arrived in the valleys of the Ogilvies from far southern wintering grounds—plovers and yellowlegs, upland sandpipers, long-billed dowitchers. One day where a small feeder emptied into the Blackstone River, we saw a wandering tattler, a species that isn't common anywhere. Another morning following a noisy, windy night during which a skiff of spring snow fell, we found a pond near our campsite alive with about 80 red-necked phalaropes. But by dusk the pond contained only the pair of pintail ducks that had been there in the first place. The phalaropes had continued to a destination farther on.

Before our supplies of both gasoline and groceries were exhausted and we finally turned southward again, we also had our best ever looks at wolverines, one of them on the gently sloping mountainside where there was also much ground-squirrel activity. We spent a good bit of time watching that site in hopes of seeing the wolverine dig out a squirrel (and there *were* fresh diggings all around), but we had no luck.

Another time we saw a wolverine moving at its usual steady pace not far below a band of alerted Dall ewes, all eyes focused on the wolverine. But it left the sheep in peace, too.

Maybe the best summary of our Dempster trip is that we never saw more than four cars in any single day and only 1½ on the average. Keep in mind that this was May and in another month an increasing number of adventuresome tourists who like to drive lonely wilderness roads would surely have been met.

Some other roads in the Yukon are well worth exploring. For example, there is the Klondike Highway, or Loop, that runs from Whitehorse (and the Alaska Highway) to Dawson City, twice crossing the Yukon River before entering Alaska and rejoining the Alaska Highway at Tetlin Junction. Another worthwhile wilderness road is the Campbell from Watson Lake (and the Alaska Highway) through the Pelly Mountains to Carmacks on the Klondike Loop. Another, maybe the most spectacular drive of all, is the North Canol Road that begins at Ross River (on the Campbell Highway) to dead-end suddenly in the Mackenzie Mountains on the Northwest Territories border.

THE BARRENS AND OLDSQUAW LODGE.
Just beyond the point where the Canol Road becomes impassable because a series of bridges have been washed out, there is a vast, gently rolling plain of alpine tundra, labeled The Barrens on topographic maps. In spring and summer the many ponds here are occupied by several species of breeding and nesting ducks and later by broods of ducklings. So many of them in fact, that on a tranquil evening you can hear their chattering from some distance. Among the most abundant and vocal of the waterfowl are the oldsquaw males with striking black-and-white plumage. These inspired our friend Sam Miller to name his wilderness guest accommodation Oldsquaw Lodge.

It was purest inspiration that caused Miller to place Oldsquaw where he did, on a knoll overlooking more than 100 square miles of undulating terrain. Right here, too, is a blend of high arctic and boreal plant and animal communities. Not one tree stands any-

Wolverines are rarely seen anywhere, but the odds of a sighting them may be best in wilderness Yukon, especially along the Dempster Highway.

Wildlife biologist Sam Miller, an expert on Yukon natural history, operates Oldsquaw Lodge (right). This on the Yukon's border with the Northwest Territories.

where in view. The vista from the lodge extends to the Backbone Range of the Selwyn Mountains in the west and to the trackless Mackenzie Mountains to the east. No power lines, no railroad tracks, not a single building of any kind mars the view. In fact the only sign of human presence other than Miller's lodge is a rutted, abandoned dirt road, the old Canol Highway, that winds haphazardly east and west, but which is gradually being erased by time and nature. The exact site of Oldsquaw is just a few miles east of the Yukon–Northwest Territories border and very far from civilization.

We first met Sam Miller when at age 40 he "retired," leaving his career as a wildlife biologist for life in the Northwest Territories. He had spent the past dozen years capturing and studying grizzly and polar bears. During the spring of 1979, with the help of friends and his brother Ed, he began construction of his lodge from scratch. Unable to transport building materials to such a remote place, Miller salvaged old bridge timbers and planks, window frames, and even some piping from abandoned construction camps on the Canol Road. Anyone reading this will be long laid to rest before the main Oldsquaw Lodge and the surrounding cabins begin to crumble.

The main lodge building rises a tall two stories high, with large windows and a deck overlooking The Barrens. Such marvelous spectacles as wolves hunting caribou have been seen from this aerie. Five two-person cabins flank the lodge, and each evening a sauna steams out back. Sam Miller finally completed the project in July 1982.

Oldsquaw was constructed for guests, of course, but long before Sam was finished, wildlife began to move

in. Arctic ground squirrels realized that burrows dug beneath the building were safer from barren-ground-grizzly bears than burrows elsewhere. Cliff swallows in large numbers took up residence under the extended roof eaves. Their mud nests, which have a tendency to break up and fall following hard rains, were built and rebuilt. Mud and droppings sometimes form a slippery mat on the deck below, which makes footing treacherous for guests studying The Barrens through spotting scopes. But Miller has never tried to evict the birds. "What the hell," he figures, "they like it here, too."

Other species of birds discovered a bonanza when Sam and his helpers caulked the spaces between building timbers. Too many found this insulation to be ideal nest-building material and have never really stopped pulling bits of it from the chinks. Miller has often pondered what the birds used before his insulation arrived.

One item from civilization that has been, and always will be, omitted from Oldsquaw is electricity. There is no roaring generator to violate the peace and wildness. In fact Peggy and I spent several days on the tundra there without noticing its absence. During the short summertime season, it is sunlit for 23 hours a day. When we retired at night, we drew the shades to shut out the brightness. Even at midnight light glinted from the countless tundra ponds all around us. As the sun descended, it was reflected like blue-tinted crystal from the surface of one pond and then another. Any heat we needed on chilly mornings came from a small wood-burning stove.

The Barrens is a ridiculous name for this landscape, which is not barren at all. Through binoculars or spotting scopes, often by bare eye alone, we could watch caribou mothers and their spring calves traveling, feeding, moving erratically, and never pausing in one place very long, as if to baffle pursuers or to escape insects. This continuous movement prevents damage to the fragile terrain, too. Grizzly bears sometimes come very close to the lodge to dig in the local ground-squirrel colony. Occasionally a moose, the males growing antlers covered with dark brown velvet, browse around those ponds fringed with dwarf arctic willow. Once a small pack of wolves passed through Sam Miller's compound, first pausing to sniff at the sauna and then near the kitchen where Irma Russell (a Belgian World War II war bride and then the cook) was baking doughnuts. They never came that close again, at least during the day, but we often heard them at night howling not far away.

Miller's intention for Oldsquaw was a lodge that would be strictly a place for naturalists and friends, a place to escape from urban pressures and concerns. And it is. But it is also an extraordinary destination for nature photographers. Besides the more visible large mammals, countless smaller creatures are easy to find, too. At least 200 species of wildflowers bloom during a normal summer, coloring the landscape, and

Miller's ability to identify each with common and scientific name is most humbling. I hated to hike out among them because each step meant trampling a weasel snout or windflower, a lousewort or moss campion.

Birders find The Barrens a particularly interesting place. During a typical morning of hiking and stopping often to photograph plants and scenes, we would count 21 or 22 of the 109 species Sam Miller has identified in the region. Most common probably are the white-crowned sparrows that are singing everywhere in summer. Venture too near to a long-tailed jaeger's nest, as we did a couple of times, and the adult birds dive and hover threateningly just before your eyes. But at least one short-eared owl left its ground nest on silent wings as we came too close and did not return until we were almost out of sight. Near one small tundra pond we found Lapland longspurs and savannah sparrows claiming territories above where a water pipit had a nest beneath the spongy turf that was no larger in diameter than a tennis ball. Lying down on my stomach, I counted three eggs inside, then crept carefully backward to avoid further alarming the parents.

Toward the end of one summer at Oldsquaw, we

The moose is the largest mammal living in the Yukon. Bulls like these are most active and visible in early September at the beginning of the rut.

A bull moose at twilight near Oldsquaw.

A gray gyrfalcon has struck a ptarmigan near
Oldsquaw Lodge and now plucks and eats it. The
gyr is the premier bird of prey of the Far North.

saw an annual phenomenon. At precisely the same
time the young cliff swallows were leaving their mud
nests under lodge eaves for the first time, a gray gyrfalcon appeared to catch easily and dine on quite a
few of the plump fledglings. In fact at one time we
counted six gyrfalcons, those most splendid of arctic
prey birds, on hand to "harvest" the season's swallows.
Later, when the bonanza had petered out, we watched
the same gyrfalcons, including some of their own
newly fledged young, hunting around the lodge for
willow ptarmigan.

Miller's guests reach Oldsquaw by two different
means. One of them is by driving the Canol Road
(Yukon Route 6) from the Campbell Highway junction at Ross River to road's end at Macmillan (or simply Mac) Pass where a few rare-metal mines operate
in summer. The name Canol comes from "Can" for
Canada, and "ol" for oil. The Canadian oil in question
was discovered near Norman Wells, N.W.T., above
the Arctic Circle, and in the early 1940s the U.S.
Government believed it needed that oil to supply
Alaska during World War II. Older readers may recall
how, despite the exorbitant cost of the project and
the bounds of common sense, it was decided to build
the Canol Pipeline and a parallel road from Norman
Wells across 650 miles of arctic wilderness, some of
it then unexplored, to Whitehorse and finally to Fairbanks.

In a feat that some compare to building the Panama
Canal, crews working from opposite ends managed to
finish the job and meet near where Oldsquaw Lodge
stands today. But neither the small-diameter pipeline
nor the road was ever used, and much of that portion
within the Northwest Territories was soon washed

away, another instance of massive military waste. Today you reach Oldsquaw by prior arrangement, or by
calling on the radio from Mac Pass. There Sam picks
up guests in a 4-wheel-drive, high-centered pickup
for the short, rough trip to camp.

Or you can fly to the wilderness airstrip at Mac
Pass. During our first visit in 1981, we caught a Trans
North Air twin-engine Otter flight from Whitehorse
to Mac Pass. The name of the company had been
changed a few days before from Trans North Transport, locally known as TNT, because owners felt the
original name was bad for business.

But a truly great opportunity for wild adventure exists out along what's left of the route of the old Canol
Road east of Oldsquaw into the Northwest Territories.
This is a trip I have always regretted being unable to
make. Using Oldsquaw as a base, a starting point,
some very strong, experienced backpackers have
completed the arduous trek eastward over the Mackenzie Range to the Mackenzie River and Norman
Wells—about 150 miles as the crow flies. This is an
almost unmatched opportunity to walk in the loneliest
of arctic mountains were the Dall sheep, caribou,
wolves, and grizzlies have seen few if any humans. I
know that the scenery is simply breathtaking because
during the early 1960s I was a member of the first
big-game hunting party (together with Frank and Homer Sayers and Jack Antrim of Columbus, Ohio, and
outfitter Bud Brewster of Calgary, Alberta) to explore
the Mackenzie Mountains and Carcajou River region
along the Canol Road west of Norman Wells.

To a considerable extent, summer backpackers
could use the dilapidated construction camps along
the way as overnight shelters. Scrap for firewood is
abundant here. Some buildings among the rusting vehicles and abandoned road machinery are still quite
weatherproof. But several river crossings where the
Canol bridges were long ago washed away would be
the most formidable obstacles, especially to careless
hikers. That, a word to the wise!

I vividly remember our most recent visit to Oldsquaw, in early September. One day it was late summer on the tundra. The next morning, we beheld
outside our cabin an astonishingly different world. In
most places summer blends subtly into autumn; here
on the edge of the Yukon Territory, autumn had exploded in a blaze of color.

Literally overnight The Barrens all the way to the
Selwyn Mountains had turned from gray-green to
glowing yellow, veined with gold, speckled with red,
mirrored in the potholes. Below us a hundred or more
barren-ground caribou paraded in a long, thin line
toward traditional breeding grounds beyond the far
peaks. White manes and antlers left red by the shed-

Herds of barren-ground caribou still roam the northern Yukon. This bull is still in velvet.

ding of velvet made the scattered bulls far more handsome than before and much easier to spot.

Peggy and I watched the caribou until they became specks in our binoculars and until a silver-tipped grizzly plodded into view in the still-low sunlight. It grazed closer and closer, until it was about 150 feet away, without seeming to notice us or the looming structure of the lodge. Then suddenly standing erect, the bruin

stared at us for a few seconds. Probably uncertain of what it saw, the animal dropped to all fours and vanished as silently as had the month of August.

Now we noticed the small flocks of shorebirds gathering overhead, in farewell flights from northern nesting grounds on their way to warmer climes far south. A hawk owl perched on the post that had served all summer as an emergency radio aerial. Like

To me the true gold of the Yukon is not in nuggets found in the ground, but in the exquisite colors of autumn. Aspen forests are luminous here on September days. Next page: Aspen leaves ornament the waterways.

the landscape, the raptor was burnished gold in the sun. A few minutes later inside Oldsquaw Lodge we ate a breakfast large enough for that grizzly we had just seen.

That was September 1985 and near the end of our fifth trip to the Yukon. During the North American autumn every self-respecting professional photographer spends as many daylight hours afield as he or she can. Although we have faithfully filmed autumn, in fact have deliberately followed fall from Denali, Alaska, to Sonora, Mexico, we have never known the seasonal foliage and the skies to be more luminous, more breathtaking than those of the Yukon that year.

The only trouble here is that the halcyon days of September pass far too quickly. Most mornings are frosty. One day toward the end of the month, the leaves on the trees fall and the stunning colors reflected on Kluane Lake and small ponds of The Barrens are gone . . . literally overnight.

Have you gazed on naked grandeur where there's
nothing else to gaze on,
Set pieces and drop-curtain scenes galore,
Big mountains heaved to heaven, which the
blinding sunsets blazon,
Black canyons where the rapids rip roar?

—Robert Service

CHAPTER ELEVEN

Wild Alaska's Future

In recent history, following a good many gains on environmental issues under the Carter Administration, there followed eight years with a Reagan government of 18th-century mentality, ignorant of or unfeeling about environmental problems facing humanity. The dismal Reagan record on the environment is especially to be deplored. Acid rain, toxic-waste dumps, contaminated water sources, and the use of poisonous chemicals became more deadly menaces every year. But clearly the president chose to channel his efforts and use his enormous early popularity in other directions.

Certainly wild Alaska has not escaped the creeping cancer of our neglect and shortsightedness. In fact Alaska's environmental problems and issues may be more evident than others because the land is so beautiful and pristine to start. Damage is easy to see, and if critical conservation battles taking place all across the Great Land are not soon won, the results will be even more obvious. One battleground as I write this is the Arctic National Wildlife Refuge, although the war is not being waged among the wolves and wildflowers, waterfowl, and caribou that live there. Instead it's being fought in the U.S. Congress where Americans are lobbying both for and against oil exploration and drilling along the coast of the Beaufort Sea. Of course it's also being waged in the hearts of those Americans who most love Alaska and wildness, who want to see that land used for its highest and best purpose, that which it now serves. Remaining untouched, the natural order will continue: caribou will migrate freely, calving on traditional grounds, blizzards of snow geese will nest, and polar bears will den inland, giving birth to tiny young each year.

Stated simply, the American oil companies believe there might be recoverable oil on the Arctic Refuge, just possibly more than 9 billion barrels. But the U.S. Department of the Interior's own report estimates only a 19 percent chance of finding economically recoverable reserves at all. And even if these *are* discovered, it would make almost no noticeable difference in the total production. What drilling *would* do is create a

Kinnikinick, or bearberry, is found throughout much of threatened Alaska. Previous page: Oil exploration and drillling along Alaska's remote and fragile Arctic Coast could severely jeopardize the welfare of polar bears, among many other species.

precedent whereby drilling would be permitted almost anywhere at all in the future. It would also inflict harm to this fragile area that could never be undone and which would never heal.

The vast Arctic National Wildlife Refuge was proposed for complete, permanent wilderness protection as long ago as the 1930s by wilderness advocate Bob Marshall and biologist Olaus Murie. Had it been so designated at that time, it would not now be in jeopardy, because wilderness areas are inviolate. In 1987 Congressman Morris Udall of Arizona finally introduced such a wilderness bill. When the Alaska National Interest Lands Conservation Act was passed in 1980, a final gift of the Carter Administration to the American people, the Arctic Refuge was closed to oil and gas development pending a six-year study and, it was hoped, forever. The Reagan Interior Department's report was the first shot fired in the battle to open the refuge to the oil companies.

There is really only one sane, ethical, long-range solution to this problem: Declare the entire refuge a wilderness. Here we are at the farthest, wildest edge of our country, rising from salt water and the coastal plain southward to the Brooks Mountains. This is the only place left in this entire hemisphere where the numberless herds of large mammals and the predators that live on them still roam free. Musk-oxen lived on these plains before and since the last Ice Age and are now making a last stand here. Over 100,000 caribou of the Porcupine Herd travel back and forth and across the Canadian border. What we might lose is far more valuable to the nation in the long run than a few month's supply of oil, which is about all we can reasonably expect to gain. Instead conservation—that is, better and wiser use of the petroleum we now have—could quickly save that much.

Even when regarded purely from the standpoint of profit, the opening of the Arctic Refuge to anything but viewing is a terrible mistake. Tourism has become Alaska's second largest source of income, increasing steadily in recent years. Current projections are for an increasing growth in visitor travel. This is just the sort of economy Alaska needs—something other than the more usual boom-or-bust industries that plague the Great Land. So why reduce this final frontier to a replica of the Prudhoe Bay oil field, which is desecrated by roads and ugly buildings, littered by rusting machinery and garbage, oil stains, and junk impossible to catalog?

There is another important point to be made here. Certainly we must be aggressive in producing domestic energy resources. Arizona congressman Morris Udall said this: "We must never forget the lesson that everyone but the Reagan administration learned during the great energy crisis of the late 1970s. That is, an energy policy relying too heavily on production, while ignoring the numerous cheap and effective conservation alternatives and alternative fuels, is doomed to failure. Without a balanced national energy policy we have no business invading such precious areas as the Arctic National Wildlife Refuge."

Future prospects for wild Alaska might not seem quite so dim if the Arctic Refuge were the only area of concern. Ominously a similar cancer is appearing—and spreading—elsewhere: from the coastal plains and fiords out into the Pacific Ocean, for example.

DRIFT NETS. Tom Jefferson of Santa Cruz, California, a biologist-observer of the U.S. National Marine Fisheries Service (NMFS) has spent time aboard Japanese fishing vessels in Alaskan waters, and what he has seen should make the blood of environmentalists run colder than the arctic seas and convert anyone who had not already seen the truth to a rabid, hard-core environmental activist.

On a typically foggy morning in the waters south of the Aleutian Islands, the crew of a Japanese fishing craft slowly pay out 9 miles of drift net from the stern of their 130-foot boat. Then while the crew sleeps, the detached, unattended net "fishes" the top 26 feet of the ocean until dawn. It is capable of ensnaring everything larger than 2 inches in diameter, the size of the mesh. Anything the size of your thumb, for example, could end up in a Japanese fish market in Tokyo. At daybreak the captain turns toward a radio signal from the buoy attached to the net, which has drifted freely and now lies 4 miles away.

It takes about 3 hours for power winches to haul the net, and then skillful, experienced Japanese fishermen extract thousands of salmon from the net. These salmon, of course, would otherwise spawn in Alaskan streams. The prized fish are easy to handle. Not so easy to disengage are the shearwaters and other seabirds, mostly dead, but a few only half dead, which are tossed back into the sea. Then come the sea mammals, in this case Dall porpoises, mostly lactating females, drowned together with their calves.

Jefferson reports that very few of the porpoises are found alive during the net retrieval. When they find themselves held fast in the drift net, they struggle and twist violently to free themselves, only making matters worse. In the end the air-breathers die.

So far scientists have been unable to determine why most of the Dall porpoises taken in the nets are females. Because the fishing season coincides with the calving period, most females, if not still pregnant, are nursing young. The result is surely a lot of orphans every July in the Bering Sea that cetologists believe will not survive.

Those sea mammals that do manage to free themselves are often wrapped in pieces of the nylon net that continue their deadly duty. Remember my mention of this injury to fur seals in my chapter on the Pribilof Islands?

There are several terrible problems here. First is the deplorable fishing method itself, and second is its magnitude. Third is the fact that it was ever permitted within the 200-mile coastal zone considered U.S. waters—or anywhere in the world for that matter.

According to Greenpeace, an international conservation watchdog group, Japan, Taiwan, and South

192

Korea operate 700 drift net vessels, fishing mostly for squid, with single nets as long as 30 miles, in Alaskan waters. As we have seen, these also kill untold marine mammals, seabirds, salmon, anything that swims.

U.S. Senate Counsel Robert Eisenbud describes these 6- to 30-mile-long pelagic drift nets as "devastatingly effective curtains of death" to marine life. He calculates that more than 20,000 miles of net are scattered over the Pacific every day, a good portion of these in Alaskan waters, intended to catch marlin and other billfish—farther south—as well as salmon and squid in the north. But of course the nets never discriminate. Anything from orcas to puffins that comes into contact with them is doomed. Because of savage weather and high seas in the North Pacific, an estimated 12 miles of net are lost per night, or about 600 miles per year are left to drift freely, buoyed by their floats, killing wild creatures as long as the nets last. And nylon lasts a long, long time. Such abandoned nets are believed to be the greatest killers of marine mammals in the North Pacific. Regulation of the drift-netting fleets is virtually nonexistent.

With a couple of rare exceptions, the Japanese have permitted no outside observers on their fishing boats.

But even a tiny sample of their work has been enough to verify a dreadful situation. One observer reported that in one month of operations the nets of a single boat killed 72 marine mammals, of which 14 were northern fur seals. Considering the hundreds of drift-net boats operating, that fur seal mortality on one boat helps account for the recent annual decline of more than 5 percent a year in the Pribilof Islands' fur seal population. During the summer of 1987 on St. George Island, resident observer Greg McGlashan showed me many seal carcasses washed ashore that had earlier been extracted from nets. Another one was pitifully dying after managing to drag a section of lost net out onto the beach with it.

On June 23, 1987, in Washington, DC, District Judge Norma Johnson issued a preliminary injunction giving the Japanese drift-net fishermen 20 days to get out of the U.S. 200-mile zone. It is believed that most boats left, largely because they already had all the salmon they could handle. But we are not really certain, because with budget cuts, patrolling our own Pacific waters for fishing violations has had no priority at all.

There are two serious problems here. In the simplest

Fur seals are among the many marine mammals and sea birds that become enmeshed and killed in 6- to 30-mile-long pelagic drift nets. Marine mammals also become tangled in torn and floating net fragments.

language, Japanese fishing policy everywhere, especially in the North Pacific, constitutes international banditry. Fleets from Hokkaido roam the Aleutian region and the mainland Alaskan coast pillaging the fisheries at will. Many were caught in violations during 1987, but most were not detected. A lot of this must also be blamed on the Reagan State Department, which was reluctant, or refused outright, to forge a realistic fishing policy with foreign governments. We desperately need fishing regulations based entirely on scientific information and our own long-term best interests.

As I write this the United States government is considering a permit that would allow the Japanese salmon fleet an "accidental kill" of 550 Dall porpoises and 450 northern fur seals in a season of drift netting. It's a perfectly ludicrous thought. The correct thing to do would be to outlaw all drift netting in our own

waters, while trying to persuade other countries to stop it everywhere else, too.

Well, you might agree that things *are* bad out there in the arctic seas, but that seems so cold and is so far away. Nobody ever travels out to see the Aleutians anyway, and the resources of the sea can stand exploitation. At least everything is much better on the Alaskan mainland, you hope, where there is a good chance you might indeed go some day. And when

you do, you'll find the forests, the mammals, the birds, and the fish all there waiting for you—Alaska as you've always dreamed it would be. Wrong. Consider the following lunatic antic of the U.S. government.

THE THREAT FROM LOGGING. First pick out a large, lush rain forest containing some of the most magnificent old trees on earth. Designate millions of acres of these trees for cutting, despite a glut of timber on the market, which now sells at rock-bottom prices. Since the value of the additional timber to be cut cannot even pay for pushing new logging roads into the wilderness, just supply the U.S. Forest Service with all the money it needs to eliminate the forest. Finally, so that taxpayers cannot complain (or maybe even learn about this tactic), make the appropriation permanent to avoid any regular review by Congress. That pretty much has been the case for the Tongass National Forest of southeastern Alaska, a land of incomparable beauty, when uncut. And the Tongass is vast, about the size of West Virginia.

In 1980 the Alaska National Interest Lands Conservation Act established millions of acres of parks and wildlife refuges. This was desperately needed legislation because that was our last opportunity to do the right thing in the 49th state and this needed doing quickly. But to win the necessary votes for passage, the Carter Administration also agreed to spend millions of tax dollars each year encouraging two timber companies to log the Tongass National Forest. Three decades before Jimmy Carter came to Washington, an earlier ill-conceived federal policy had persuaded two pulp-processing companies to set up shop in the Tongass. Pressure by them "to save the timber industry of the Panhandle," and by the apparently perennially short-sighted Alaskan politicians, succeeded in inserting a provision that has now come home to endanger a large part of Alaska.

Specifically that provision requires the U.S. Forest Service to spend whatever is necessary to build roads in this steep country that will allow loggers to chop down 450,000 million board feet of lumber a year from the Tongass. This is no ordinary forest—much of it is hemlocks, spruces, and cedars, bearded and moss-covered, many 800 years old. When they are felled, nothing like them can exist to thrill the next 20 generations of humans. As you read this a Sitka spruce 100 feet tall and 20 inches in diameter breast high

Forestry practices in southeastern Alaska, especially in the Tongass National Forest, are both wasteful and costly to American taxpayers. They have an adverse effect on commercial and sport fishing by ruining salmon spawning streams. Road building in these public forests should be stopped.

yields about 1,000 board feet. This 1,000 board feet is selling for about the price of a hamburger!

By law Uncle Sam is now paying out $40 million per year on the loggers' behalf, while receiving only a few cents on each dollar in fees or from timber sales in return. The tab to the taxpayers by 1987 exceeded $360 million and was accompanied by consequences of three awful kinds.

First, the awesome forests that serve as watersheds and that tourists want to see are being eliminated. The same Japanese that pillage our fisheries are able to buy timber at bargain-basement prices to produce products (rayon, for example) that compete with our own. The federal government of the United States does not even require that this timber be milled in the U.S. by workers in Alaska. Rather it allows timber to be sold whole—as "round logs."

Unable to distinguish the American public interest from private interests, the Forest Service defended this logging as a "jobs program." The southeastern Alaska timber industry does indeed employ about 1,900 men, but it also endangers, and is certain to jeopardize more drastically in the future, two other important industries: tourism and commercial and sport fishing. People will not visit Alaska to see eroding mountainsides of stumps. Logging can also have a deadly impact on fishing by its degradation of salmon spawning streams. Soil washed into streams covers the stony bottoms where salmon eggs develop.

Southeast Alaska annually adds almost $150 million to the state's economy through commercial fishing for king, coho, sockeye, chum, and pink salmon. Bottom fishing for crab, shrimp, and halibut plus recreational angling raises that revenue to $200 million annually. To maintain that income, it is vital that spawning streams for salmon be pure, cool, and unclogged by silt and logging debris. Consider the case study of a typical salmon river compiled by Bart Koehler, executive director of the Southeast Alaska Conservation Council.

The Lisianski River is among the more productive wild salmon fisheries of southeast Alaska. According to the Alaska Department of Fish and Game, the Lisianski's pink salmon run is fished every second year for an estimated catch value of $900,000. In addition, the Lisianski River annually produces an estimated $46,000 catch value of coho salmon. (This coho value is only for fish caught within Lisianski Inlet itself).

Although commercial fishing industries in the United States and Canada are regulated and well managed to assure a sustained catch far into the future, fleets from Asian countries fish almost without restraint and sensible limits. Their impact on fisheries and marine mammals is terrible.

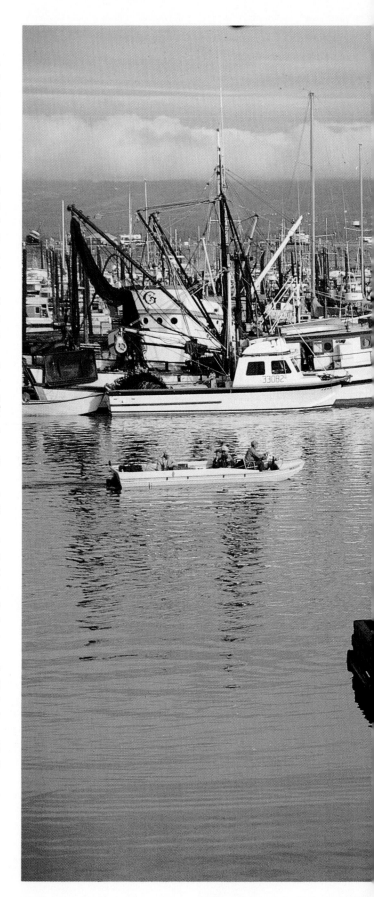

196

These catch value figures do not include the indirect economic benefits to fishermen, suppliers, communities, etc. Put in an annual perspective, the Lisianski River is worth $446,000 a year *at the very minimum*, with very little cost in public funds. It should also be noted that these figures do not take into account the recreation or subsistence-use value of the area, nor its value for sport hunting and sport fishing.

The Forest Service had plans to log 20 million board feet of timber along the Lisianski River corridor during 1986–90. According to agency figures, the cost in public funds for actual management expenses for logging the area would have ranged from $3–$4+ million. This included expenditure of over $1.6 million for the main permanent roads—not including temporary spur roads. These figures did not include any other costs, such as opportunity costs for the loss of subsistence, recreation, natural, and fish and wildlife values.

Using current stumpage prices, the 50-year contract holder for the area, Alaska Pulp Corporation in Sitka, would have paid an average of $2 per 1,000 board feet for the Lisianski timber. For a cut of 20 million board feet, the Federal Treasury would have seen a mere $40,000 in receipts! Outrageous.

In other words, the Forest Service would have expended $40 million of public funds to manage logging of the Lisianski River and damage the fishery with 21 stream crossings and a number of cutting units adjacent to the river for a return to the treasury of only $40,000. Instead they could have protected the Lisianski River corridor in order to maintain the existing productive fishery which, in a natural state, produces well over $400,000 per year.

Fortunately, a great public outcry stopped logging in the Lisianski for the 1986–90 period. However, it has no permanent protection at this time and will again be on the chopping block in 1990. The Lisianski River deserves to remain a *wild* fishery with no logging and no roads. Public support for adding this area to the West Chichagof–Yakobi Wilderness for permanent protection is growing. Certainly, long-term protection of the Lisianski River is the best use of the area and is, without question, the best investment for the public.

Top left: This iris was blooming just outside our tent at McNeil River. Near left: We found this pasqueflower growing beside a trail near Riley Creek, our first wild bloom of the season at Denali. Next page: We photographed the yellow paintbrushes while hiking along the sandy shores near Yakutat. Normally flower photography isn't hazardous, but here the place was full of fresh brown-bear tracks.

America must stop pandering to logging interests in Alaska by eliminating the fixed expenditure for logging. The sooner Congress legislates against this environmental and economic scandal, and the president signs the bill, the better.

Even if the Tongass scandal should be corrected, there are other problems in wild Alaska that range from nagging to serious that must be addressed.

The midsummer wildflower show on the Pribilofs is exquisite. There lousewort is among the most common blooms.

200

OTHER THREATS. In July 1987 the oil tanker *Glacier Bay* struck a rock in Cook Inlet, and 125,000 gallons of crude leaked into the sea. In a sort of super-cleanup effort, the U.S. Coast Guard was eventually able to soak up and contain most of the damage, but for a while it appeared that commercial fishing in that area might be wiped out. Fortunately it wasn't, but the threat of a similar, larger spill elsewhere—one that cannot be contained—is always a frightening possibility.

Especially when world gold prices rise, the rate of placer mining accelerates on likely gold-bearing streams all over Alaska and the adjacent Yukon Territory. There are no solid figures available, but the cumulative effect of thousands of placer-mining operations on the landscape, on river watersheds, and on gamefish in those rivers might be tremendous. We need hard data on the effects of this practice, whereby tons of stream bottoms are displaced daily, and perhaps restrictive legislation.

So what is a reader to do?

My first suggestion is to see the Great Land for yourself. Explore the splendid parks, float the wild rivers, escape into the bush, fish the salmon streams . . . all this to experience the matchless treasure for yourself. See if you don't agree with me that this mostly still wild state is too precious to lose. Ever.

If you do agree with me, become an Alaskan activist, no matter where you live. Keep in touch with doings in that region. Join one or more of the national conservation organizations to keep abreast. Write any of the following organizations for membership information:

The Sierra Club, 730 Polk St., San Francisco, CA 94109

National Wildlife Federation, 1412 16th St. NW, Washington, DC 20036

National Audubon Society, 950 Third Ave., New York, NY 10022.

Wilderness Society, 1400 Eye Street, NW, Washington, DC, 20077

National Parks and Conservation Association, 1015 Thirty-first St., NW, Washington, DC 20007

The Nature Conservancy, 1800 North Kent Street, Arlington, VA 22209

Greenpeace, 1611 Connecticut Ave., NW, Washington, DC 20009

Alaska Environmental Lobby, Inc., P.O. Box 22151, Juneau AK 99802

CHAPTER TWELVE
Photographing Wild Alaska

When first assembling and editing the photographs for this book, my conclusion was that Peggy and I had done a pretty good job. I figured that the slides well illustrated the wild Alaska we had explored so many times. But on further consideration I recalled the far too many great photo opportunities we had missed.

I sadly remember, for example, the pair of bull caribou fighting on a ridge overlooking Wonder Lake in Denali National Park; both of our cameras ran empty, just when the bulls went head to head. The caribou broke off the instant we were reloaded. Some other unhappy memories include missing the precise moment a gyrfalcon struck a willow ptarmigan barely 40 feet away (too slow on the shutter release); the time I hiked after Dall rams to the top of Denali's Primrose Mountain with too few rolls of film in my pocket; the day on Afognak Island when we *almost* drifted to

A long-focal-length telephoto lens makes it possible to capture Alaskan creatures such as a bald eagle (left) and (above) a greater scaup.

We spotted this cow moose from the road and were able to get into action quickly because we always drive with cameras at the ready.

within a few feet of sea otters preening on a rocky islet (but the boat scraped a rock and frightened them); the wolverine that circled and then stared for several minutes into my open tent in the Yukon (while the nearest camera was outside on a tripod); the cross fox kits I was photographing as they gamboled by their den (when another person appeared and frightened them inside); and the time I dropped a Nikon F3 camera body off a cliff.

Half the pleasure of being in wild Alaska can be in photographing the experience. This chapter aims to help anyone do a better job of it, and that includes avoiding the pitfalls and making too many mistakes. Much though can depend on plain old good or bad luck.

In earlier books of this series (*Erwin Bauer's Deer in Their World, Bear in Their World, Horned and Antlered Game, Predators of North America*), I discussed basic photographic techniques and outdoor cameras in detail. In this book I'll write of both, but only as they pertain to Alaska. I'll also give you a look at new equipment on the market.

CAMERAS. All of the photography in this work was done with 35mm single-lens reflex (hereafter called

SLR) cameras, which I consider to be the only practical choice for active adventure and wildlife work. Of course larger format systems can be used for excellent results, especially for photos of the magnificent scenery. But the larger the format, the more difficult transport becomes and the less mobile you become. To Peggy and me the utmost mobility is very important.

The advantage of the 35mm SLR camera is that it is fast and easy to use. As well, it is reliable if properly maintained and comparatively light in weight. Most of the better brands are rugged and dependable. On each photo trip we carry four or five camera bodies, all of the same system so that each one can accept any of the lenses we own. Components are completely interchangeable. The reason for the extra camera bodies is twofold: first, to have spares handy in case of mechanical failure and, second, to have a fully loaded body handy when the action is fast and one runs out of film at a critical moment. This happens more often than the laws of probability would seem to dictate.

All of our camera bodies are equipped with built-in exposure meters and motor drives to advance film automatically. A motor drive is invaluable in wildlife photography, eliminating the distraction and additional step of advancing the film manually. With the motor drive the photographer can concentrate instead on focus and the action in the viewfinder.

As I write this many professional photographers are gradually converting to autofocus cameras and lenses. With these you can theoretically forget about critical focus (as well as advancing the film) and concentrate solely on the subject and composition. One of our cameras is now an autofocus and under certain conditions works very well. It freezes many action subjects in sharp focus much faster than is possible manually, and the green point of light signaling perfect focus is reassuring when we are in doubt.

With autofocus, a beam of infrared light emitted from the camera bounces from an object in the center of the viewfinder, returns to the camera, and activates a motor that precisely adjusts the focus. Unfortunately it bounces from the object closest to the camera, often a twig or blade of grass rather than the intended subject.

Recognizing this problem, and also the fact that the subject looks better when not in dead center of the photograph, the manufacturers have installed a focus lock. With this you focus the beam directly on the subject, lock the focus, then re-aim the camera as you choose. The disadvantages here are obvious. Wildlife subjects often move in the instant between autofocus and re-aiming the camera, resulting in a lack of good focus. In these cases it's quicker to focus manually. In addition the autofocus will not work when the background is reflective (as when birds fly over shining water), when there is little contrast between subject and background (as a polar bear in the fog), and when all background lines are horizontal. The magic beam likes vertical lines. Fortunately, these autofocus cameras can be used in manual-focus mode too.

However, the autofocus cameras and lenses are cheaper than other cameras and are becoming increasingly available as manufacturers phase out many of their older, manual models. Certainly in time some of the autofocusing problems will be solved, but that time has not yet arrived.

LENSES. The lenses affixed to our 35mm SLR cameras are what make or break our pictures in Alaska as anywhere. Only the photographer's own technique and composition have as much effect on picture quality as the capability of the lens. To shoot the land-

Peggy and I use just a few of the many lenses here for nearly all of our wildlife photography. The large lenses in the back row are all Nikons; left to right they are 600mm f/4, 80–200mm zoom f/3.5, 400mm f/3.5, 200–400mm f/4, 300mm f/2.8. The small lenses and accessories in front, left to right, include the following: Nikkor 55mm f/3.5, Vivitar 5600 flash, Nikkor 35–70mmf/3.5, Vivitar 70–210mm f/3.5. The two small lenslike accessories at the extreme right are tele-extenders.

When you are using lenses longer than 200mm, a sturdy tripod will give you better chances of getting tack-sharp photos. The tripod all but eliminates image-blurring lens shake. Rain gear for camera equipment is vital.

scapes of Denali as well as close-ups of the wildflowers, the brown bears, and nesting shorebirds, more than one lens is needed. For this book we have depended heavily on the following lenses: a 55mm f/3.5 macro; a 35–70mm f/3.5 zoom; an 80–200mm f/2.8 zoom; a 100mm f/2.8 macro; a 300mm f/2.8, a 400 f/3.5, and a 200–400mm f/4 zoom. And on other occasions a 600mm f/4 telephoto lens was invaluable.

The 55mm and 100mm macros are those we've used for close-ups of wildflowers and lichens, mushrooms, and berries. I suppose we've used the 35–70mm zoom most to shoot Alaskan landscapes. Our 80–200mm zoom telephoto is the one we like best for large mammals that can be approached to fairly close range. This means it's not the best for bears, of course. The 80–200mm is also ideal for photographing animals in their natural habitat, rather than full frame where the animal alone is emphasized. On recent Alaskan trips, the 200–400mm zoom telephoto has become our workhorse for wildlife photography. With the 200–400 a wild subject can range from near to far and back again while we adjust its relative size and position in our viewfinder.

Some very good photographers do not share either our high regard for, or our dependence on, so many zoom lenses. In fact even the finest zooms today may not be *quite* as sharp as lenses of a single focal length. But the greater versatility—carrying only two or three lenses rather than twice that many for the same range of opportunities—more than makes up for the possible loss of sharpness.

Besides our lens selection, each of us also carries a 1.4× tele-extender or teleconverter in a handy pocket. Inserting this between camera body and any lens instantly increases the focal length of the lens by 140 percent. In other words, 200mm becomes 280mm, and a 400 becomes a 560mm.

FILM. Three kinds of color positive or slide film were used to shoot our Alaskan photographs: Kodachrome 64 and Kodachrome 200 (which is 2½ times as fast as 64) and Fujichrome 100. We usually underexpose all these about one half stop for better, deeper color saturation. Sixty percent or more of the pictures were taken with Kodachrome 64. We relied on the Kodachrome 200 mostly when light conditions were poorest; in fact this film is especially useful in Alaska during the frequently dull light conditions. We shot

Fujichrome largely as a comparison or backup because in certain light conditions, Fuji gives brighter, more attractive color. I especially like the green in Fujichrome on damp, dreary days.

TRIPODS AND SUPPORTS. If you spend any time seriously photographing in Alaska, you will absolutely need a solid camera and lens support. Many fine pictures are taken with a monopod or with one of the fitted camera stocks (similar to gunstocks) available today. It is also possible to get by simply by resting a camera on anything from rocks and tree limbs to auto windowsills. But eventually you need, or should have, a sturdy tripod. And the longer the telephoto lens you use, the greater the need for the tripod.

By all common sense, the tripod I depend on is too heavy for someone anticipating a 70th birthday to lug up mountainsides or to use as a wading staff when fording a cold river. But a field tripod for use with a camera and telephoto combination weighing up to 10 pounds must be sturdy if nothing else. Sadly, those able to do the job are heavy. Mine, having each telescoping leg made up of three sections, scopes down to 20 inches and can be set up fairly easily on irregular or steeply sloping terrain. Each leg is separately adjustable higher and lower, inward and out.

As important as the three-legged stand itself is the tripod head on top. Ours are identical ball-type heads that allow smooth panning in all directions with a minimum of adjustment. Both have quick-release mounting features so that cameras and lenses can be affixed or detached in seconds. Also, with the identical heads, *all* our equipment remains interchangeable, not just the cameras/lenses.

PROTECTING AND CARRYING GEAR. Perhaps more than anywhere else, photo success in Alaska depends as much on other equipment as on photographic gear itself. I have seen great Alaska photographs taken with simple cameras, even with today's budget automatic cameras that are a fraction as expensive as ours. But without waterproof carriers or containers for whatever the equipment, you can soon run into serious problems.

Carrying photo gear is the first consideration and there are several choices, none of them the chic shoulder bags that have proliferated in catalogs and camera stores. For traveling by air or by car, camera equipment is best protected inside aluminum or plastic waterproof and dustproof cases that can be locked. If going by air, these cases should be carried by hand, never as checked baggage. Individual items are cushioned and separated from one another by plastic foam.

In the field, I see the choice as among a belt- or

You can buy a tripod Monoball head with quick-release feature that allows you to change lenses or camera bodies with a turn of a knob and an easy slide-in and slide-out maneuver.

Alaska's spongy land and interlacing streams make hipboots a handy, sometimes essential, item.

fannypack, a photovest or jacket, and a backpack. The selection depends on the distance to be covered and the amount of gear to be carried. Nothing beats a beltpack for a short hike or climb to shoot scenes or closeups, with no need for a tripod or long telephoto lens. Most of the photovests on the market handle a surprising amount of gear in individual zippered pockets or compartments. One manufactured by my friend Leonard Lee Rue III, in Blairstown, New Jersey, is made of camouflage cloth, has 19 pockets, shoulder loops for a spare camera, plus a plastic drop seat for sitting down on wet ground. This vest makes any photographer mobile, yet fully supplied with equipment.

Probably because it's difficult to teach old dogs new tricks, I favor the same exterior frame backpack in Alaska in which I have lugged photo and camping gear from the Andes to the Himalayas in Kashmir and almost all the way to the peak of Mt. Kenya. It does not have as many compartments as the vest, but has more cargo space overall. Besides the camera stuff, it will hold a rainsuit, insect repellent, matches, snacks, a plastic canteen and water purification apparatus, and sunglasses.

Tough, zip-lock plastic bags, more than it seems we might ever need, are handy in our van or in the field in Alaska. Suffice it to say that you would be foolish not to have protection for everything in a land where the sun does not always shine.

CLOTHING AND FOOTGEAR.
Weather determines what we wear. I can remember an August day in Denali Park when frost covered the ground in the morning. But by midafternoon I had stripped down to a T-shirt on a mountainside overlooking Toklat Creek because the temperature had risen well above 80°F. So dressing with the layering system is sound advice. No matter how promising the day when you start out afoot, carry a warm jacket and foul-weather suit.

More than once, as strange as it may seem, a small umbrella (large enough to cover lens and camera) clamped onto my tripod has been valuable. I have tried many different kinds of plastic covering or wrapping for equipment to permit shooting in rain or wet snow, but they do not permit camera operation as well as the umbrella that collapses into a package no larger than a small telephoto lens.

Our foul-weather suits, always close at hand in Alaska, consist of hooded parka and pants combinations designed for bicyclists and therefore of tough, very lightweight material. These are quite expensive but outlast several cheaper suits.

Waterproof footgear is essential. Period. An Alaskan photographer needs either knee-high rubber boots or calf-high leather boots that have been silicone impregnated. Too much of the landscape is spongy or laced with streams to wear the dry-country boots that are serviceable elsewhere. Also we carry lightweight hipboots or western-style irrigation boots. We've needed them on every trip to Alaska.

PREPARED TO SHOOT.
The best way to make the most of any trip to the Great Land is to always be ready to shoot. That goes for traveling the highways by car or tour bus, as well as when hiking, climbing, or even exploring coastal fiords by kayak. One of the fine opportunities we missed by *not* being ready came just outside Anchorage early one morning. A fine bull moose crossed the four-lane thoroughfare and then stopped to stare back at passing traffic while standing belly deep in the wildflowers of the Eklutna Sanctuary. Wildflowers grow everywhere during Alaska's summer, but nowhere in greater profusion, probably, than here. Certainly in no place as accessible. But by the time I retrieved my camera from underneath other duffel, the moose had wandered far away. It was a bitter lesson.

So now it's our firm policy to always have at least one outfit, a camera with an 80–200mm lens ready at all times—with longer lenses within reach. We also try to have lens and shutter speed set on the exposure that will most likely be correct. Having extra rolls of film in each backpack, parka pocket, and elsewhere is also cheap insurance against missing a great shot.

Many of the pictures in this book were made in marine environments, often from a boat, because some of Alaska's best wildlife spectacles are at the edge of the sea. While photographing from some kind of watercraft can take you closer to certain creatures than approaching them from overland, it also causes special problems. The constant motion—the impact of waves, swells, and tides—is the most troublesome factor, but usually the motion can be tamed.

Although the impulse may be to crowd to the front of a tour boat, perhaps to get a closer look at sea lions on a rocky beach, it is wiser to photograph from as near the *center* of *any* boat as possible. That's where motion is least. The greatest movement is at each end of the craft. Even when drifting on fairly calm water, we use shutter speeds of at least ½50th second, and ⅟500th second if the exposure permits.

Small, moving subjects such as the rock sandpiper (top right) pose a focusing challenge, requiring continual focal adjustments via the lens barrel. The short-eared owl at right cooperated nicely by holding still and turning broadside to allow sharp focus on its entire body.

This river otter stood still for focusing, yet the great distance and long telephoto minimized depth of field, allowing tack-sharp focus only on the animal's face.

FILTERS. A polarizing filter (one of the two most useful filters in color photography) can be valuable in marine photography because it reduces or eliminates surface reflections, the objectionable white hotspots, while making pale skies a deeper blue. Polarizers are most effective when used at a 90 degree angle to the sun, but they cannot, unhappily, change dull gray skies to pleasing blue.

Speaking of filters, the other very useful one is the graduated filter in which one-half is clear and the other tinted. These are most useful when one-half of the image is much darker than the other, as when the rocky island full of sea lions in the foreground is much darker than the sky behind. Since color film cannot "see" the same range of contrast as the human eye, the photo, without the filter, will either be exposed for the seals with the sky far too light, or the sky will have a reasonable light value, but the seals and rocks much too dark. The filter helps reduce the contrast to a level that the film can manage. In this case the tinted portion of the filter should be gray. These filters can also be tinted gradually to pink, orange, blue, or green and used to enhance sunset photos, but unless used with discretion, the results are garish and unnatural.

LOCATING AND APPROACHING WILDLIFE.

If you confine your work to Alaskan state and national parks, to sanctuaries and wildlife refuges where hunting is not permitted, you will find that most wildlife residents—especially the larger mammals—tend to be more tolerant, with some notable exceptions, than elsewhere in America. Hunting with a camera is possible anywhere, anytime in the state, but obviously your chances are immensely reduced where hunting is done annually. We therefore have spent 90 to 95 percent of our time in Alaska in the places where wildlife is protected. That's good advice for anyone.

Because of the great variety of big-game species—caribou, moose, blacktail deer, grizzly, black and brown bears, Dall sheep, goats, walrus, wolves, and (introduced) elk, Alaska and the Yukon are the premier places in the New World to trophy-hunt with a camera. So challenging that it can become addictive, this is a sport with no closed seasons, no bag limits, and no licenses to buy.

During my first photo adventures I was content simply to shoot increasingly better pictures of the big-game animals I met. But more and more Peggy and I have found ourselves trophy-hunting, looking for bull moose and white sheep rams bigger than any we

I never try to sneak up unseen on an animal such as the bull moose above or the arctic fox (white phase) at right. Peggy and I try to stay in full view so that our quarry can see us while feeding without looking up. We never approach an animal directly, and we try to avoid eye contact. We move gradually nearer our subject by angling toward it, pausing often and changing course, trying to appear as other, noncompetitive creatures on the landscape.

have seen before. More than once the strong probability, or even just the possibility, of locating a trophy has pumped new strength into tired legs and has made some mountainsides not quite so hard to scale. I have made more than my share of extra footprints on the landscape just for a closer look at a big bull or a ram standing on a distant ridge. Serious trophy hunters with gun or camera will understand what I'm saying here.

But no matter whether the target is a rutting male moose or a cow caribou with a newborn calf, knowing exactly how and when to approach requires a combination of patience, care, common sense, and knowledge of the species' behavior. Even in sanctuaries some species become more tolerant of people than other species do. As a rule, large animals are less wary of photographers the longer they have been protected. Denali is anyone's best bet anywhere, for example, to find moose or caribou within photographing distance. Still, each individual animal has its tolerance limit. This is an invisible boundary beyond which a sensible, serious photographer should not pass. Otherwise the animals will quickly move to a great distance and thereafter keep to that longer range.

There is no possible answer to exactly how close an animal can be approached. But for clues, watch the eyes and ears, the hair on the neck, and the tail of any antlered mammal, and you will soon know its intentions. Nervous or agitated ones flatten ears, appear uncertain, start grazing or browsing quickly, or if close enough, nudge one another before clearing out. That's a good time to back off and use a longer telephoto lens.

I never, ever try to *sneak up* unseen on an animal on foot. That would be useless anyway because the senses of all are keen enough to know when a human is getting into photography range. On the other hand, Peggy and I make an effort to stay in full view so that our targets can see us without looking up. I believe it's most important never to approach an animal directly or purposefully, and also to avoid eye contact, especially prolonged eye contact. Rather Peggy and I move gradually nearer to our subject by angling toward it, pausing often and changing course, trying to appear as other and noncompetitive creatures on the landscape. Day in and day out, that is what works best, at least for us.

BEST WEATHER. For more than three decades I have gone to Alaska or the Yukon whenever I had the time, the invitation, or merely some faint excuse. But if I were given the choice today, I would consider the seasons of spring and late summer–early autumn

as the most rewarding. The winter days are just too short. Summertime is fine for wilderness fishing, but this is also the period when the most visitors crowd the wildlife areas.

We have always enjoyed our best and brightest weather early in spring, when the new green vegetation improves any photograph. Yet in autumn the landscape is the most stunningly beautiful—a time when a trophy hunter should spend every hour possible in the field in search of rutting activities. But in fall we have also suffered through much more bad weather—days totally lost—than in other seasons.

TOURS AND TRIPS. From all the foregoing, planning a trip to wild Alaska–Yukon may seem bewildering. But it need not be. One solution today is the photographic or nature group tour. Every summer a growing number of travel agencies, adventure clubs, float-trip companies, and professional photographers offer all-expense tours of from two weeks to a month to many of the best wilderness and wildlife destinations. I'm not writing now of the typical tours that feature the towns and gold camps, the saloons, salmon bakes, and the Alaska pipeline, maybe with a one-day bus tour of Denali National Park. I mean, instead, group trips tailored for wilderness and photography people.

There are limits and disadvantages to these, of course, namely the lack of complete freedom to stay as long as you like, or to leave when you choose. Also, nature photography is not really a social pastime. One or occasionally two compatible photographers working together can accomplish much, while just one or two additional people might drive the wildlife away. Many wild creatures do indeed become increasingly fearful in direct proportion to the number of people drawing near.

But almost always the advantages outweigh these drawbacks. Most group trips we've encountered are well planned and led capably by Alaska experts who are skilled photographers or vice versa. Trips are scheduled to take greatest advantage of peak periods; you go to the Pribilof Islands or Round Island, for example, when the most fur seals or walruses are on hand. Accommodations and/or camping gear, plus all meals, are provided. All flights and boat trips are booked. Usually the only hitches are the result of weather, which outfitters cannot control. Each member of a group pays less for travel than he would if going alone. When travelers are inexperienced in the bush there is safety, both real and imagined, in numbers.

Two of the top group trip operators in Alaska are Joseph Van Os of Van Os Nature Tours (P.O. Box

A photo blind can come in handy. This portable Ultimate Blind from Rue
Enterprises, Blairstown, New Jersey, is very light and compact when broken down.
Setup takes only a couple of minutes.

655, Vashon Island, WA 98070) and Victor Emanuel Nature Tours (Box 33008, Austin, TX 78764). Both of these companies have long experience and are moderately priced and reliable.

BEARS. I have saved for last the important matter of bear photography. No adventure to Alaska–Yukon is really complete, fulfilling, without meeting bears. But it is absolutely vital to meet them at a distance that will not get anyone, bruins or people, into trouble.

Of course a bear might be encountered anywhere in the 49th State, except on a city street. But the odds of suddenly coming upon a dangerous bear anywhere are infinitesimal. My guess is that every year far more people are killed by jealous spouses than are even threatened by bears. Still, a person venturing into the backcountry should be aware of the potential of a bear encounter. And photographing bears greatly increases the odds of such a meeting.

Being in bear country demands discipline and cautious behavior, especially if you are in grizzly or brown-

bear territory. No matter what else we are doing—hiking, fishing, photographing ground squirrels or glaciers—we watch studiously or constantly for bears. I never want to be surprised by a bear, nor do I want to do the surprising. Whenever we do see a grizzly, we give it a wide berth. When out in the bush we do not walk whistling or ringing bells because in some areas such noise may simply indicate that a fresh supply of chocolate candy bars and granola is on the way. Besides, a bear can usually hear the footsteps of anyone who is or is not carrying a bell. And in many cases, a bear's nose gives it the first notice anyway.

The importance of always keeping a clean camp cannot be overemphasized, even though we realize that earlier campers in the same spot may not have done so and may have accustomed bears to seek food there. So look for the cleanest campsite you can find, especially if in a tent rather than a hard-sided vehicle. Avoid being near obviously slovenly campers. Do not cook or store food in the same tent in which you sleep. Do not sleep in clothing you wore when cooking because clothing absorbs food odors. When leaving your

No matter what we are doing in Alaska, we watch constantly for bears. We never want to be surprised by a bear, nor do we want to do the surprising. Bears near their food caches and mothers with cubs are particularly dangerous.

vehicle in known bear areas, keep the windows tightly closed and the doors locked, although other humans are far more likely to break in than bears.

Except from the security of our vehicles, or when within easy reach of it, we seldom try to shoot mother bears with cubs—and never from close range. Even more ridiculous would be to step between a female and her cubs. A mother grizzly is among the most determined of all wild animals to protect her young. Never play games or take chances with any bears.

As I wrote in *Erwin Bauer's Bear in Their World*, stay in the open when in bear country as much as possible, so that you always have the widest, unobstructed view all around. I am doubly alert when walking into a wind, especially a steady, high wind, because that is the one situation in which a bear might not catch your scent or hear you until too late. Only a fool walks in grizzly country without watching for such fresh sign as tracks, diggings, and droppings. In late summer and fall we never walk unheeding through patches of berries where bears might be feeding.

If you ever detect the unmistakable foul odor of decomposing meat or see an animal carcass while on the trail—stop. Retreat. You have found either a food cache or what will soon be a bear's food cache, so stay away. Black bears, as well as grizzlies and browns, can be evil-tempered and aggressive when food is involved. If the animal carcass you find is covered with leaves or ground litter, you can be absolutely certain that it is a bear food cache and that the owner is nearby.

Some faint evidence exists that odors other than those of food and cooking attract bears. Among these are perfumes, scented deodorants, and sweet-smelling lotions. So it seems sensible to avoid them just in case they are indeed attractors. There are also indications that human body odors, sweat and urine, for example, may repel bruins. But don't bank on it.

In a number of studies and analyses of bear attacks, one fact seems evident throughout. Very seldom do bears attack more than a single person. Maybe the animals are simply intimidated by a larger mass, but there are few verified instances of bruins taking on a group of people close together. So it does make good sense for photographers to form small groups when working near the animals.

I know of no guaranteed lifesaving methods for dealing with aggressive bears, although a few tactics have proven to be better than others. Remember that a bear suddenly standing up on hind legs is probably not showing aggression, although it may look more intimidating in this position.

A bear moving its head up and down or slowly from side to side may simply be trying to get a stronger

Although some people carry firearms, we choose not to. Guns are forbidden in national parks. And handguns are forbidden everywhere in Canada. They're also heavy. We use caution instead.

scent or a better view—and nothing more. The best response most of the time is to stand still and to try speaking to the bear in calm, even tones while slowly backtracking. *Slowly.*

One thing *not* to do is cut and run . . . unless an easily climbable tree or your car is near enough so that you can reach it safely. Remember that a bear is faster afoot than the world's swiftest human sprinter. Don't forget either, that any black bear can climb better and faster than you can and that some grizzlies are able to climb a considerable distance when tree branches are favorable. In addition, running can actually stimulate a bear to give chase when it might not otherwise do so.

In Alaska carrying a backpack full of equipment has saved several outdoors enthusiasts from serious injury. One possible response to a threatening bear has been to slowly, calmly (I know it's difficult to be calm in a position like this) remove the pack, set it down, and back slowly away—don't run. The separated pack really has distracted the animal long enough for the hiker to make a getaway.

But not removing the pack also has prevented more

terrible injury and saved a life or two. With no other escape, and a bear almost upon you, the best, last resort is to play dead. Drop to the earth face down, drawing your knees up to protect chest and stomach. Clasp your arms around your head with your hands around the back of your neck. With the backpack thus shielding much of the torso, hikers have emerged from repeated attacks with the most serious damage to their equipment.

FIREARMS. Some writers have advocated carrying firearms whenever in grizzly country. Guns are correctly forbidden in national parks, which settles the matter for these places. But how about elsewhere? There are good and bad arguments, both pro and con.

Admittedly there have been times on lonely Alaskan mountainsides when I would have felt more comfortable and secure with a sidearm. But usually I am already carrying more weight than a sensible senior citizen should be toting and don't relish the thought of more. I'm also convinced that some men might behave more arrogantly and with less caution in bear country if armed. Many animal behaviorists are convinced that the more intelligent wild creatures, which include bears, are able to detect one's intentions, probably even one's fears. Thus an unarmed photographer *might* have better odds of capturing natural bear pictures than one carrying a firearm.

In any case, Peggy and I have opted to exercise extreme caution near bears rather than carry a weapon. So far we have not regretted the choice. I should add here that handguns, no matter how carried, are illegal in Canada. It is a criminal offense simply to carry one in a car en route from the lower 48 through Canada to Alaska. Border guards make a very thorough search of vehicles bound for Alaska.

INSECTS. So what is more dangerous than bears in wild Alaska? Mosquitos, for one thing, especially for anyone planning to roam the tundra regions and the northern half to two-thirds of the state. A few parts of Alaska are surprisingly almost free of these insects, but it is foolish to wander in the bush without a sufficient supply of repellent. On still, hot summer days in the far north, you may need a headnet and gloves as well. At times blackflies can be far worse than even the mosquitos.

CARE OF EQUIPMENT. For photographers, two other dangers can be even greater than mosquitos: moisture and dust. Constant effort is required to fight both of them. Dust may seem an unlikely enemy where

Campground bums such as the gray jay offer good practice in camera handling and yield treasured images as well.

precipitation is high. But given just a day or two of dry weather, many unpaved roads become dust bowls. Because of both these extremes of dust and moisture, it is essential, no, critical, to keep all equipment covered. Here is what we suggest.

To clean all lenses, first use a blower brush or ear syringe to remove all surface dust. Avoid using "canned air" as the cold spray may damage optical glass. Next use lens tissue to clean the optics. Use a good quality lens tissue, NOT a silicone impregnated tissue commonly used for cleaning eyeglasses.

The lens tissue should be first folded into three or four layers. Next moisten the tissue with lens-cleaning fluid. Holding the lens tissue by the edges, clean the lens from the center outward using a gentle wiping motion. Repeat this process a couple of times until the lens is clean. The condensation from your breath on the lens surface will indicate any remaining debris. Once the front lens surface is clean, repeat the process on the rear surface of the lens and on filters.

On a quiet evening during our last trip to Alaska, Peggy and I sat in camp on the Teklanika River in Denali Park drinking hot coffee while cleaning our lenses. The setting sun tinted the clouds and the river's calm surface pink. This was a scene we had often enjoyed. Soon we would be driving homeward, more than 2,000 miles back down the Alaska Highway, leaving what now seemed a second home far behind. We then regretfully realized that no matter how many more times we returned to the Great Land, we would never be able to see or photograph all of it. But as surely as gold flecks the river bottoms and bears roam the tundra, we'll try.

Index